BEING WHOLE

HEALING FROM TRAUMA AND RECLAIMING MY VOICE

CASSANDRA FAY LECLAIR, PHD

Edited by Stephanie Hataway & Corrie Knight

Cover Design by Maria Stoian

Front Cover Photograph by Pauline Stevens

Photographs of Cassandra by Evan Kay

Kintsugi Bowl by Kintsugi Gifts UK

To Alexandra and Kellen,

You are integrated into the deepest fibers of my being and woven into the center of my heart and soul.

Thank you for your unwavering love and support throughout all of our traumas, crises, and hardship.

I am honored to be your mom.

I love you.

I am the person I need to be for this stage of my life.

Silence will no longer hold me hostage.

This is my journey to reclaiming my voice.

Being Whole is a fractured memoir about a healing process. It is cyclical, repetitive, and fragmented. Not unlike the healing process can be for many of us.

My story is not linear and may seem disjointed if you try to read it as such. I invite you to immerse yourself in the process. Try to imagine how your mind works as you experience crisis, trauma, or stressful events. In these pages, I strive to unravel that process and heal from my disordered thinking and destructive patterns.

As you read *Being Whole,* you will notice pieces that keep reappearing. You will recognize examples that cut across contexts. You will feel how things can go forward, backward, and stay in the same place. You may reflect upon your own experiences and see how you have created your own patterns.

Being Whole is a work of nonfiction. This is my survival story, and all events have been recalled from my perspective. The methods referenced herein may not work for everyone, and the content of this book should not be used as a substitute for consulting licensed medical professionals.

INTRODUCTION

This was never a story I planned to tell, and for many years, I worked hard *not* to tell it. I pushed it away, built walls, and developed a number of strategies to ensure it would stay safely hidden away. But life circumstances eventually jolted me into the realization that I could no longer contain this experience. I felt propelled by a force larger than myself to tell my story, and one day, I started writing.

As a child, I endured years of sexual abuse. And I did not tell. For decades, I kept that secret hidden from everyone, including my parents. Consequently, I bore not only the deep emotional scars from the abuse but also the profound burden of this terrifying and devastating secret and its accompanying, gut-wrenching shame. Recognizing, acknowledging, and dealing with the abuse and its fallout seemed insurmountable for many years.

Ironically, most people would describe me as a very open person—maybe even too open—

and it's true. I was an open book in many ways. I spoke freely about my infertility, emotional abuse, lupus, disability, and divorce. With all of that, what else could there be? I'm sure no one guessed there was more, but I had carefully edited my story, and there were missing chapters that I had, essentially, locked away in a vault. A vault that resided deep inside of me. These stories would never see the light of day— or so I thought—and remained hidden for more than thirty years.

During the time I carried this burden, I was constantly paralyzed by fear and panic. Appearing seemingly out of nowhere, the debilitating fear seized me and overwhelmed my emotional and physical resources. All it took was one word, an event, or a memory, to hurl me through time and space, forcing me to relive the worst of my abuse while my body tried, desperately, to protect me by launching into a surreal fight-or-flight state that left me emotionally drained and physically exhausted.

This fight-or-flight response combined with my inadequate means of coping left me feeling mentally weak, unstable, and out of control. I hated myself every time it happened. I learned to retreat and withdraw from relationships to avoid burdening others with my troubles. I often isolated myself, in part out of self-protection, but also to shield others from what I perceived as my weaknesses and flawed character. Keeping many relationships on a surface level helped me avoid any emotional space where my patterns might become noticeable to others. This dysfunctional dance helped me cope, while I desperately tried every available form of therapy, medication, and healing modality to break the patterns and deal with the emotional fallout I was experiencing.

After going to school, reading, researching, teaching others, and going to therapy—more times and varieties than I can count—I understood that not talking about my abuse, and my utter brokenness, kept me from being free. A virtual prisoner of my secrets and shame, I expended enormous amounts of mental energy reliving and being re-traumatized by these horrible memories and their accompanying feelings. The concept of wholeness did not exist for me. In a desperate attempt to cope, I developed many disordered thought patterns and behaviors. I was getting by, but in no way, did I feel healed and whole.

Ultimately, I had to move away from seeing myself as messy, broken, chaotic, and flat-out unstable to realize my own value and self-worth. Of course, the multitude of challenges I have experienced changed me and altered my course, but I learned that I *could* be free from my old thought patterns and actions. Confronting life-long destructive behaviors and disordered thinking required enormous effort. But every bit of that hard work was worth it for the result of finally seeing myself as whole. Being Whole. That is what this book is all about.

Being Whole tells the story of how I gathered up all the broken pieces and worked toward wholeness. I am not broken. I am whole. All the bad things that have ever happened to me

have shaped me as a person, but they do not define me. I refuse to be defined by fear, hate,

or shame.

I have arrived at a place where I recognize and appreciate that we can take whatever has made us feel broken and build something stronger, and something more beautiful and resilient, with all those broken pieces. So many of us, maybe all of us, in ways great and small, have the potential to be like the beautiful kintsugi pottery that graces the front cover of this book. Once broken, now whole, but in a stronger, more beautiful form.

This is a story about my life but, in these pages, I chose

not to explore the abuse and other events in great detail. My goal is not to trigger readers or get overly graphic. It is about coming to a place of healing that is so profound to me that I want to use my story and my experiences to inspire others along their own healing paths. It is my belief that we can gather the broken pieces and move forward to a life that no longer feels shattered beyond repair.

There may be people who feel they bear responsibility for not recognizing some of the crushing events described in these pages. There may also be individuals who think I have recalled things in a way that is inaccurate. There might even be those who believe I am being overly dramatic and attention-seeking. Concerns like these once prevented me from sharing my truth. That time is gone.

I will share my story. I will use my voice. I will encourage others to do the same in a way that resonates with them.

I am a Communication Studies professor. Yes, you read that correctly. My purpose in life is to teach others to communicate; to use their voices to enhance their relationships and their professional lives, with effective communication. It is my heart's desire that my story can encourage and help others in their own process of healing and wholeness.

In my classes, I ask my students to take things personally. This means that if I am going to work to keep up to date on research and form new lectures, I want the theories to matter to them. I want them to take what I say and apply it to their relationships. So, in many ways, I have been healing myself one semester at a time for several years.

I have been in a very privileged position where I get to hold safe space for a variety of individuals as they make their way through life. I set up my classroom experiences to foster and encourage interpersonal reflection and relational growth. This has been my mission for a long time.

I believe in the value of human communication. I believe our voices carry us through all of life circumstances. We have to look at our inner voice, our self-talk, and our internal dialogue before we can properly discuss our communication with others. That is what I do for a living.

It also happens to be what I needed to do in my daily life that helped me heal.

Sharing this story is partly about me acknowledging there is a process. Unfortunately, there is no "Ten Easy Steps to Heal from Trauma" type solution—at least not one I have found. As wonderful as it would be if healing were a perfect linear path, this was not my experience. I visited and revisited many events and details. They were intertwined and overlapping. Experiencing the same things repeatedly, and in different contexts, brought me to a place where I finally understood my truth. Consequently, my story might seem repetitive at times. There were many twists and turns until the pieces finally fit together, allowing me to revisit them in a completely honest and understandable way.

Healing required enormous sacrifices of time and energy. It forced me to take a year off from my active social life. I needed to curate other areas of my life to fit it all in. I did not get to—

even temporarily—retire from, raising my kids, financially supporting our household, managing chronic disease issues, or any of the other pieces of my life as a busy, stressed-out single mom. At times, healing seemed like a luxury I could not afford. Never enough time and certainly not enough money, yet I made it happen anyway.

I had to.

Because I was scared every day.

Because I could never feel peace.

And I could no longer live that way.

The themes in my book represent patterns I painstakingly unearthed during my healing process. Painfully aware of some of these cycles, I was shaken by others when I realized what they represented. I repeatedly returned to my journals to figure out what kept tripping me up and what I did not understand. During this exercise, I discovered several areas where I required more healing. Upon realizing that, I dug deeply and kept working to break through every wall and barrier I had carefully constructed.

Eventually, I reclaimed my authenticity and reunited with my authentic self.

This is about connecting our spirits again.

It is about all the broken pieces coming together ever so beautifully.

It is about *Being Whole*.

Being Whole to me does not mean that I have it all figured out or that you must have it all figured out. It means we are willing to see the potential for how it all fits together. A word of caution: just because you are whole does not mean there will not still be broken pieces. Some of those pieces are sharp. I worked on healing my traumas and have even taught about healthy communication for decades.

I convinced myself I was completely healed.

I was wrong.

My healing journey will continue. There have been many stressful situations, crises, traumas, and relationship road-bumps over the years. There will surely be others. If and when new hardships and traumas present themselves, I will face the situation head-on. I am no longer afraid of breaking forever.

Again, I present my story in hopes that it will help others, but I am not a licensed mental health professional, and I do not provide counseling services. What I am is a person who believes in the power of using your voice. I know my story will not exactly mirror your own, but I hope that through the sharing of my experiences, you will find the courage to share yours, in whatever way you choose. My goal is to create space for more stories to be shared. I want to be on a path where we move forward and heal, where we acknowledge the past—no matter how painful—and recognize that our stories, both good and bad, have value.

I am acutely aware that my experiences as a highly educated white woman may not resonate with everyone. That is one reason why I wish to use my experiences and work with others through their own experiences to get a continued and better understanding of how to help people heal. I can only speak to my own lived experiences, but in doing so, I also hope to honor yours. The things that make you who you are. The things that make you whole.

> I do not want to speak for others.
> I want you to share your truth
> on your terms
> and in your own way.

At the end of each chapter there are sections called "Messages for Moving Forward." I have included them as text, but they were originally posted on social media. These are parts of lectures I have presented, and they also served as reminders for myself while I was healing. They are quotes and descriptions which dovetail with the patterns or themes found throughout the book, meant to serve as reflective reminders.

Finally, I offer this book to all the broken people. Reclaim your pieces, work through the splinters, heal the cuts, and make yourself whole.

You are more than your darkest moments.

Your life has purpose.

You are valuable.

Your voice matters.

With love,

Cassandra Fay LeClair
October 2019
New Braunfels, Texas

BEING BROKEN

*T*errible things have happened in my life, leaving many broken pieces inside me. They do not define me, but together they make me whole.

It took me a long time to see myself as whole. I beat myself up about all the broken pieces I held inside. Then, I tried to own being "beautifully broken" or "uniquely damaged," but those concepts simply did not resonate with me in any type of meaningful or useful way.

Despite working so hard at healing, I still possessed broken pieces with jagged edges that were continually shifting. The pieces were fragments of traumas I had not yet healed. They were always there, reinjuring me with their sharpness and piercing new flesh each time. Trying to heal the brokenness and fixing the pieces became my only goal, but I didn't really know how to do it.

So, I pushed the pain aside, as best I could. I tried exceptionally hard to make it not matter.

But it did matter and it was impacting me on levels I did not recognize.

Consequently, I have fallen apart many times, probably

more than most people. I have often been fragile, emotional, overly sensitive, and easily overwhelmed. These traits made me feel broken and weak. Now, I embrace the idea that accepting our sensitivity and any other perceived weaknesses is a strength in itself. I realize I do not always have to explain myself or justify my choices.

And neither do you.

For me, this is not about external validation or even confirmation of awesomeness. It is about sharing my story, acknowledging the reasons I do things, recognizing my patterns, and discussing how I processed my deep personal trauma.

We are all made up of different events we carry with us throughout our lives. Each experience, in some way, transitions into the next. Though many things have happened to me, I have always managed to recover and move forward. Then, one unexpected event shook me to my very core and led me to revisit everything.

Suddenly, situations I had recovered from were no longer tolerable. Even wounds I had healed needed more attention and deeper processing. Events I had tucked away would no longer be placed in the shadows.

I had to deal with everything that had ever happened to me.

I had to go back.

MESSAGES FOR MOVING FORWARD

You Are Not Broken

Times of trauma, crisis, and stress impact us all in different ways.
Do not judge your pain based on what another has experienced.
Each event has brought you to this moment.
You are not broken, even if sometimes
it feels like it in every way imaginable.
The dark times should not overshadow every other facet of your life.
Fill the cracks and holes in with gold.
Feel your strength.
Find your center.
Breathe.

THE CRASH

*I*n 2018, my life was going pretty well. When compared to the seven previous years I had endured; one could even call it amazing.

I had overcome debilitating illnesses. My children were thriving socially and academically. I was in a healthy, long-term romantic relationship. And, after years of being on social security disability, I had made plans to go back to work full-time to a job that I love.

I was starting to feel like myself again. I allowed myself to relax—a little. I was back in therapy and developing a solid meditation practice to make sure I was keeping myself mentally as strong as possible. I had a glimpse of what I had been searching for all along.

I had moments of peace.

I was crushing it. I was back on my path.

Then, in the blink of an eye, it was gone.

The drunk driver appeared from out of nowhere. His car hit us on the front driver's side and sent us spinning into the next lane where we were struck by another vehicle on the front passenger side, right where I was sitting. Somehow, we escaped with minor physical injuries. When I look at pictures, and see my mangled car, I am incredibly grateful. I know angels were protecting my family that night.

April 1, 2018—in addition to being April Fool's Day—was Easter Sunday. We spent the day with my boyfriend's family, relaxed at home for a while, and then went to see a movie. On our way home, we were talking and laughing. My boyfriend was driving; my son was in the back seat on the driver's side, and I occupied the passenger seat. My daughter was at home. Even though she was not part of the crash, she was still deeply impacted.

We left the scene of the crash shaken, but not in a panic. For me, though, that would all change very quickly. The next morning, I was still and sore, and my neck hurt a great deal. To be on the safe side, I decided to get checked out.

More concerning was my mood. I was anxious. I was hyperalert. I felt overwhelmed and panicky. My emotions were raw. Every defense was heightened.

I no longer had an operable car, so I asked my boyfriend to drive my son to school. After dropping him off, we went to an emergency room to get checked out and then went home. I was told I had a minor concussion, was prescribed short-acting anxiety medicine and pain medicines and told to rest. I went home, laid in my bed, and cried. I sobbed hysterically. I was in a free fall.

When the feeling had not subsided a few days later, I returned to the same ER. I was scared. I knew I was in trouble. I could tell my nervous system was in overdrive and my defenses were ratcheting up. Yet, I found it impossible to articulate what I was feeling.

I wanted to disappear. I wanted to run. I needed to escape. What was this feeling?

TERROR.

The feeling was terror, and, it was one I knew all too well. That was how it started.

Again.

That is how my life unraveled.

That is the event that led me to break down.

I was scared. All. Of. The. Time. But my fear was not just about being in the accident or even being in a car. I felt internal panic. I really can only describe it as terror. I was so afraid, and I knew I had a reason to be. Yet, it was a familiar feeling that also had nothing to do with the crash. I felt it deeply.

In my heart.

In my gut.

In my soul.

It permeated my being.

Then?

The real crash happened.

My body had been working long and hard to keep me safe. It could no longer hold on. My mind was too rattled. My system too much in shock. Everything was right at the forefront of my memory.

And just like that, I was six years old again.

Suddenly, long tucked away visions and memories flooded to the surface in a swift, dark, and horribly painful manner. They ripped through my being, tearing my soul apart. Pieces of memories crystallized with vibrant clarity, their pain hitting me with such force. I was unprepared for those memories to resurface. I was not ready. I did not want to see that space. Yet, it would not go away.

The door.

The cold floor.

The darkened room.

The basement.

The place.

The man.

I begged for my mind to stop. *Please put everything back into that hidden compartment of my mind. Please don't make me look at these pieces*, I screamed inside.

Please. Please. Please.

STOP!

It did not stop.

FUCK.

FUCK.

FUCK.

Now what? My mind raced. My heart pounded. How could I go forward when every carefully constructed wall crumbled? And, those walls protected me. How could I keep going? How would I raise my kids, go to work, pay my bills – or simply exist – when I literally could not move because the depths of my soul had been pierced? That space was complete and utter torture.

Torture I had already lived through.

And then I knew. I knew I had to go back. I had to go back and explore and uncover those memories to release them once and for all. I had to learn not to shove them away. So, I dove headfirst into the darkness.

That car crash was a catalyst for ripping everything open and revisiting old wounds; years of different traumas and turmoil I convinced myself I had dealt with. I had thought about all of the different events. I had talked about most of them openly. But I had never gotten rid of them. I carried them around without release, spending precious mental energy concealing, hiding, and ignoring their existence.

There was one big piece that never got space, yet simultaneously took up all the space in some deep part of my subconscious. The drunk driver took me back to a place where I was scared. All the time. I knew I could not live with that feeling. I finally understood where it came from.

For a good portion of my life I had suffered with anxiety. After the car accident, that anxiety showed itself in a new light. It was a palpable, mind-numbing, all-consuming fear. I finally recognized that for so long, I had medicated or attempted to talk away the pain, without ever addressing or exposing the root cause. I halfway healed those broken pieces over and over, through therapy, meds, and any other method I could find, but I had not gone back to process where it originally began.

Even though I have been through things that I think are much more damaging, somehow that was the defining moment. The crash was the thing that made all the broken pieces become

too much. It was not the worst trauma I have experienced, yet it was the one event that sent me into a place I had never visited. It propelled me back to a dark place of panic and shock with tremendous force.

Maybe it was because I had a legitimate right to be afraid that others could recognize and see, so it was easier for me to accept how much fear I had? I acknowledge and understand there are others who have experienced even more horrific events. But that is another thing about crisis or trauma—you never know what will tip the balance too far. It may seem like the smallest trigger, but it might be rooted back to something deep.

We do not get to decide when another person has reached their breaking point. We do not see how different events may have impacted them.

When we were hit by that drunk driver, it gave me a reason to be afraid that I could name and explain. I realized that is what I had been feeling on so many occasions, for so long. I did not know how to name it as fear before, because I had spent so long convincing myself that I was not afraid. I spent so much time pretending certain events did not matter, I would not even allow myself to feel true emotions about what had happened all of those years before. However, the crash reignited my fear in a very real and powerful way.

I will never thank the drunk driver. His choices impacted my life in ways that I will process for many years to come. The financial, emotional, and physical strain from the crash felt like it would break me for good. His actions caused emotional distress for my family which, in turn, caused me to reel with anger.

The type of anger that rose up was a familiar feeling and I hated it. I knew this from somewhere, yet I still did not want to address it. What was I unraveling now? I kept cycling. I had to identify the anger at the root cause. It all kept going back to what I had not healed. The common thread? I was, once again, paying for someone else's terrible choices.

I never could have predicted something like this would be the catalyst that led me to look at old events in a new light. How long had I missed these signs? I was in a tailspin, and I knew, for sure, I never wanted to experience this again.

Every horrible thing that had ever happened to me bubbled to the surface with a vengeance, and I knew I could not continue in that way. Living with that feeling was no longer an option. I had to wake up and understand why these things kept happening to me, but more importantly, I had to learn how to accept parts of my story from which I had long disassociated.

After the crash, memories of the sexual abuse I had experienced as a child hit me head on. I was so shaken that I essentially stopped all communication with friends. I shut down my social media and tried to disappear. I dove deep into several types of trauma therapy, sought many different emotional healing practitioners, and dedicated myself fiercely to the task of finally putting the pieces all together. It was an incredibly difficult and scary time.

Acknowledging the fear and succumbing to the memories was a huge defining moment in my healing. It really made me go back and begin to excavate things I had buried deep within. I knew I had to rip apart every experience and dig in to figure out how to process every crisis that had ever happened on a deeper level. I needed to do the work to heal on a more complete level overall. I had to make myself whole.

MESSAGES FOR MOVING FORWARD

Let Your Fear Become Fuel to Move Forward

I have been paralyzed by fear.
I have allowed fear to overwhelm me physically and emotionally.
I have held myself back because of fear.
I have spent most of my life beating myself up for these traits.
I hated myself every time I allowed fear to win.
You have the power to control fear.
You can tame that beast.
Do not give fear permission to live inside your heart.
You are more than your darkest moments.
You are loved.
You are safe.
You are whole.
Release your fear.

SEXUAL ABUSE

*W*hat I lost: My innocence, my self-worth, my sense of self, and my ability to trust.

I was six years old.

I grew up in rural South Dakota. I have a mom and dad who are still married to each other. I have an older brother and a younger sister. My parents owned a bowling alley in a very small town about five miles from my house out in the country.

The town was like many others in the area, full of hard-working, caring, honest people. People who would look out for each other and let you know if something was not right. People who were not inherently suspicious of others, in part because so many families had lived there for generations. To a certain degree, people knew everything about everyone.

It was a place you should feel safe, protected, and well cared for. Yet, for me, it became a place of fear.

My parents worked very hard. Being self-employed is no easy task, and I applaud anyone who can keep an establishment going. Especially in a rural area. They were successful at keeping the business running and thriving. Over the years, they both worked additional full-time jobs in an effort to make a better life for our family.

I spent a lot of time in that four-lane bowling alley. I went there most days after elementary school and had chores like sweeping the gutters, refilling the candy shelves, and washing the dishes. My favorite thing was running the cash register and learning to count change. We spun around on the counter stools, danced to songs on the jukebox, and sometimes got to eat frozen pizza for dinner. It was a wonderful place where I have countless happy memories. Plus, my birthday parties were awesome!

We did have amazing babysitters on many days, but we also were at the bowling alley a lot. Anyone with a family business will tell you that is the norm. I was not neglected—far from it. My parents knew the days at the bowling alley could be long, so they created a special space for my siblings and me to play in the basement. It was pretty cool that we could play while they were at work. As a parent now, I know how hard those years are too. Childcare is expensive and, sometimes, even small moments of time are better than going days without seeing one another.

We often played in the basement after completing our homework and chores. We had a large table with attached benches where we often played school. We could roller skate in a circle around the big bench that sat in the middle of the open room. There were toys and books and music. At one point, my dad even constructed a small balance beam so we could practice gymnastics. So much about that time and space makes me smile.

Although we had this wonderful space, the bowling alley was a place of deep conflict for me, because that building contained not only the joy and magic, but also overwhelming fear. I loved being there, in so many ways. I was with my family, and they made me feel safe. If I was with them, I was never in danger. So, how can a place be so magical, yet so horrible?

Because of a man.

Because of a man with powerful words who people trusted.

Because of a man who was a predator.

Because of a man who repeatedly molested, raped, and psychologically manipulated me.

For years.

The back room.

The dark door.

The concrete floor.

One hand covering my mouth, while another rubbed me over my clothes—at first. Like some sick and perverted ritual meant to calm me down. He would continue, softly brushing my hair out of my face, almost tenderly, while he thrust his other hand inside of me. He was never mean or threatening then; instead, he tried to reassure me.

He said I would be okay if I would just relax. It was confusing to hear loving words that were spoken during the horrific, hateful actions. His threats were laced with compliments. The messages he imprinted on my subconscious seemed impossible to erase.

Even now, if I have an unexpected trigger, there are times when I still have to take deep breaths and remind myself to be present in the moment. Those moments are far and few between now and they pass as quickly as they began. However, because I pushed things aside, I did not begin processing my trauma until I was thirty-nine years old.

I was six when the grooming began.

The worst of the physical abuse occurred between the ages of eight to ten.

The touching began as friendly hugs from a man who pretended to be kind. I knew I did not like him, but I did not know why. He was a prominent man in town. His family had more money and more power than my own. He reminded me of this repeatedly, especially as I said no or threatened to tell.

There was a long period of time where my dad worked for him to supplement income from the bowling alley. My abuser made sure that I was aware of the power he possessed and his ability to wield it over my family. He said he could fire my dad and make sure no one came to the bowling alley. I felt scared. Everything he said made sense because I was a child, and he was an adult. In a classic abuse pattern, he exploited the immense power differential between us, and I was utterly helpless.

My abuser was an expert psychological manipulator. He provoked immense fear in me. I believed—so completely—that I would do more harm than good by telling. I wholeheartedly convinced myself that I was the only one who needed to suffer. That I should suffer. And that sick, sadistic man exploited my desire to protect my family.

When I reflect on those days, I naturally wish I had told my parents. Even knowing what we know now about grooming and predatory behavior, so much still gets overlooked. My parents are not to blame. There is truly no way they could have known. I cannot go back and fully explain my silence. At age six, I was not equipped to deal with anything I was feeling or to understand what was happening to me.

By the time I was twelve, I decided I was going to do whatever I needed to do to prove him wrong. I decided to become strong enough to handle anything. I even learned to handle having him thrust himself inside of me. When he raped me, I would feel physically ill, but I lay there and closed my eyes and pretended to be somewhere else. Anywhere else.

When my period began, the abuse stopped. In some sick and disturbing way, I felt discarded. Though, it should have been the happiest moment of my life, and I did feel a sense of relief, it exposed a gaping wound right in the pit of my stomach. It was a horrific realization of what all he had done.

It made me sick. I felt deeply disturbed. I had suffered to prevent others from hurting and now I was hurting. I was also angry at myself. Why didn't I tell? Why hadn't I made him stop?

Who would have faith in me now? Who would believe that I stayed silent for years? I needed to tell. I wanted to tell. I wanted him to pay. But because I had accepted his words, I was convinced that if anyone found out, I would be destroyed. I thought it would be a negative reflection on me.

I believed everything else he said. I felt unlovable. I believed that all anyone would see is what I had—according to him—allowed to happen. If I had thought for one second about telling, that thought was gone now. I had been used, beaten down, and tossed aside.

I knew in that moment that he was so right. Who could possibly want me now?

That man never hurt me when my dad was there. I think he knew my dad would have killed him. My dad would still kill the man if he were alive today, and I am glad he is dead. I do not know how many other people he hurt, but I do fear there are others. I know there were a lot of secrets that stayed in families with no consideration for the other lives that were destroyed.

I owe everything to my family. It is hard to imagine how I would have made it through what happened to me without their love and support. The abuse that I suffered is one reason why I am so committed to advocating for kids and young adults to have that same love and support. I am dedicated to helping people learn how to name their emotions and communicate about their feelings. I want to continue to explore ways to help individuals process their traumas through sharing their stories, in their own way, when they are ready.

There are probably still pieces I have probably locked away. However, the memories I reflect on now have softened edges that fit together with all the other pieces. Now when I see them, the fear is gone. I feel peace. I am no longer afraid —just at peace.

MESSAGES FOR MOVING FORWARD

You Have a Story to Tell

I am a survivor of childhood sexual abuse.
I was 39 before I could say those words out loud
and speak clearly about everything that happened to me
without being retraumatized.
Remaining silent was damaging me in ways I never realized.
I had to take a big step and work through the events of the abuse.
Writing, speaking, and sharing my truth
has been the hardest thing I have ever done.
Yet, it has led me to the greatest peace I have ever known.
I no longer possess fear, worry, or panic about what happened.
You have a story to tell.
Speak your truth.
Use your voice.
Share your truth.

UNLOVABLE, UNWANTED, UNWORTHY

*F*ear. Guilt. Shame.

Words that became themes. Themes that became patterns.

What does it mean to be truly unlovable? As a child, I did not know for sure, but I knew it was the last thing I wanted. I still do not know what it means really, but I know that truly believing you are unlovable is a dark and scary space.

My abuser told me that no one would ever love me. Doesn't that sound obvious? I mean, you have heard it before, right? Classic abuse rhetoric. I can still hear his voice telling me those horrible words. He looked me right in the eyes and made this pronouncement in a strong, steady tone. His voice did not waiver. He appeared confident and gave the impression of someone who did not believe he was wrong in any way.

I am sure if I saw it all now, I would be able to pick up on cues that I missed as a child, but hindsight is 20/20. I had zero clarity beyond his words. He spoke them emphatically. Convincingly. Hauntingly.

Thankfully, when I picture his face, that room, or any of the memories now, I recognize and realize how ridiculous and wrong it was.

Then? I believed him.

I bought into it deeply. He was exceedingly convincing. I was exceptionally scared.

Whenever I expressed disbelief or threatened to tell, he would devise new ways to coerce me to remain silent.

There was one memory in particular that was very hard to confront. It took a long time to sort through every way it has impacted my life, to untangle the web I created by internalizing his words.

When I defiantly cried out that my parents would still love me no matter what, he took his message a step further. He stood over me, looked me right in the eye and told me, clearly, authoritatively, persuasively, and disturbingly:

"No one will ever love you because of what you allowed to happen."

He told me that I was no good and that no one would want me.

"You will never be able to give anyone what you have given me. What you allowed me to have."

What.

The.

Fuck.

What I allowed to happen?

What I allowed him to have?

Oh my God.

I felt sick to my stomach.

I could barely breathe. I had allowed it to happen. He was right. It happened. Over and over and over. I never said anything. To anyone. I held it inside all the while thinking I was keeping other people safe with my silence. Trying to take all the pain so no one else would have to hurt. And there I was with his words seared in my brain.

I was unlovable because I had allowed this.

Those words ripped right through me. My throat clenched, I couldn't scream, shout, or even sob. I was frozen. I no longer had a voice.

I was responsible.

No wonder my stomach hurt so damned much. No wonder I had problems with emotional regulation. No wonder I blamed myself for *everything*.

My God.

What kind of horrible person says that to a little girl?

To anyone?

That memory, that *lie,* was foundational for so many things in my life. Occasionally, I still need to say the words out loud to remind myself:

It is not your fault.

Blaming myself is my go-to. It is my nemesis. I have allowed myself to be unhappy across so many contexts, thinking I was always the root cause. It took me many years to feel I was worthy or deserving of anything other than blame.

Every time I confronted that memory, I experienced intense physical reactions. My throat would begin to close, my heart would race, and my chest would feel tight. Tears would well up and my nose would tingle. I felt my stomach sink, and I wanted to puke.

I could not breathe.

I could not speak.

I wanted to shut down.

I wanted to remain silent.

I wanted to forget.

It hurt—badly. So very badly.

But I had to confront it, tackle it, and isolate it repeatedly to work through those emotions. Shutting it out again would not solve anything. It would have been much easier to stop, but then I would be stuck. I would be right back there.

Again.

Is it any wonder that I teach about using your voice? As a Communication Studies professor, I have made it my mission to help my students talk through situations and learn healthy communication practices. In part, perhaps because I remember feeling so deeply aware that my voice could have saved me. I felt like I failed myself all those years ago.

I had to keep going this time.

I had to reclaim my voice.

Because I accepted blame, I internalized shame. That shame made me feel worthless. That shame made me feel darkness. That shame made me not care what happened. I felt that I was unworthy, undeserving, and all around unlovable.

I can write and talk about it now without panic, but sometimes stray tears will emerge and trickle down my face. Now, these tears comfort and cleanse. I see it as a release of a bit more toxicity.

He said I was unlovable. He made me feel pleasure and then told me it was my fault. That is one of the disturbing and confusing things about abuse. You can still feel pleasure, even when you are terrified.

This is one of the things that doesn't get talked about very much. If someone is repeatedly touching a pleasure center, eventually, you may feel something. Maybe not every time. But even if it happens once, it is complete and total mental anguish.

Even when others were around, he hovered over me,

there with a hug or a command to sit on his lap, but never in a way that drew too much attention or when anyone might become suspicious. Always complimenting me in a way that made me feel sick. When he would happen to catch me alone in the basement, I squirmed and tried to get away. He covered my mouth and spoke softly and gently.

Eventually, it became some sort of soothing tone. I knew he would do whatever he felt like and, if I stayed quiet, it would be over more quickly.

At some point, I stopped feeling like I was even there.

But then, when he was finished, he had ways of jolting me back to reality. He reminded me again that my parents would think I was unlovable because he could tell I enjoyed it. Writing that sentence for the first time made me wince. At first, revisiting those thoughts brought panic and shame. These themes and messages were all incredibly painful to work through. I truly have no comprehension as to how someone can willingly cause another such intense pain.

He told me I was beautiful and special, but no one else would think that about me if they knew. So, I had to keep the secret. He told me that my family would have nothing. So, I had to keep the secret. He told me that no one would believe me because I didn't say something sooner. So, I had to keep the secret.

I did not want anyone else to experience pain. I had to keep this pain to myself or others would suffer. I had to stay silent or I would cause pain for others. I knew how much I was hurting. I truly could not comprehend hurting anyone else.

The blocking out, the shutting down; it caused me to fracture so much. I no longer trusted my feelings. I was very young and did not know how to interpret things. Pleasure that was also scary? Loving words that were accompanied by horrible actions? That is an incredibly dark and distorted reality in which to live. I was confused and had no way to externally process what I was feeling.

I felt lost.

It is Not Your Fault

For the majority of my life, I have lived with deep shame.
I carried immense guilt,
because I felt responsible for the horrific actions of others.
My abuser said it was my fault.
I believed him.
I carried around the weight of his words.
I internalized blame for every bad situation that happened to me.
The shame overpowered me.
It left me riddled with anxiety, depression, and guilt.
If you are a survivor of abuse, neglect, or assault,
I want you to know it is not your fault.
Even if you didn't speak up. Even if you didn't press charges.
Even if you still haven't told a soul.
It is not your fault.
You did not deserve the terrible actions that were inflicted upon you.

You are valuable.
You are loved.
It is not your fault.

LOSING MYSELF

$\mathcal{S}$o, again…how does this all happen? How do you go through life and get things so twisted up? How does it change your thought patterns so deeply? I took his messages and imprinted them on my core. They were not my beliefs about myself, but I adopted them and made them my own. I accepted his version of me, all while rallying against it internally.

I was confused.

I was scared.

I was angry.

But it was also the pattern.

Say what you want about patterns, but at some point, they become routines. You know what routines feel like? Safety. I was stuck in a cycle and trying to escape it felt terrifying. My whole world was collapsing already, but at least I knew what it looked like. Doing anything different? Adding another unknown element? Risking more turmoil? Nope. Not going to do it. I can just keep quiet.

When the abuse stopped, I hated the attention of men.

But I also craved it. I had very deluded and misconstrued ideas of what love meant and what men wanted. He stopped trapping me in that basement back room when I was in middle school, when I got my period. How supremely messed up is that?

I assume I had aged beyond his sick, pedophilic tendencies. Maybe it was too risky. Fear of pregnancy? Fear of my growing desire to scream and cry out about his evil deeds? Maybe he could see how close I was to telling everyone.

I do not know. I just know that the abuse ending should have been the most glorious thing.

It was physically freeing, and it was mentally torturous. Who was I now? I thought he said I was so special. He destroyed my life, my sense of self, and stole my self-worth. He walked away without suffering one bit.

Even after the abuse stopped, he found ways to make me feel small, insignificant, and dirty. He made comments about other men taking their turns now. He said he saw the way they looked at me, but I should remember he looked at me first. I felt disgusted.

I wanted to be loved. I was trying to keep that in the past, yet there he was, reminding me of it with his physical presence while destroying my mind with his words again. I fell into that cycle and pattern and chose the wrong people to give my heart and body to. I wanted attention from men, yet that attention left me feeling empty. Being desired felt thrilling, yet lonely and horrible.

As the years went on, I craved and needed love and acceptance, particularly from men. Again, it was as though I had to prove my abuser wrong. I needed to show myself—and in some twisted way, him—that men would love me.

Would want me. Did want me. Even after everything that had happened and all that I had endured.

But I was confusing the two—being wanted and being loved. They are not the same.

MESSAGES FOR MOVING FORWARD

You are Worthy of Your Own Respect

Communicate to yourself with kindness.
You are worthy of your own respect.
The self-talk we engage in has the power
to change how we view ourselves.
Negative thought patterns can creep in to our conscious
and destroy our sense of self and can harm
our relationships with others.
We teach our children to talk nicely to others.
We need to do better than that.
We need to teach them that kindness starts
with how they talk to themselves.
We need to focus on positive self-talk at younger ages.
It is never too late to retrain your brain.
Start with small steps each day.
When you do say something negative about yourself, correct yourself.
Give yourself grace.

Do not beat yourself up in times
when you catch yourself being negative.
That is only adding more negativity!
I don't care if you have to compliment yourself for small daily tasks.
Start there.
Tell yourself you are awesome because you got out of bed.
Congratulate yourself for being on time to work.
If you start to give yourself accolades for small accomplishments,
positive self-talk becomes the norm.
You are worthy of your respect.
Be kind and compassionate.
To yourself and others.

ESCAPING

*M*iddle school was the absolute worst.

I am not a medical doctor, but I am pretty damned sure that lupus was already rearing its ugly head way back then. I was often sick. I missed a lot of school. I lost a lot of friends. I did not acknowledge the abuse and was unaware how it was impacting me. I thought constantly about what had happened. I had no idea how much it was stealing my energy and happiness.

I tried to flee even before high school. I completed a long summer program at a school in Bethel, Maine. I loved every second. I even convinced my parents to let me apply for that fall, my freshman year. I received scholarships and they found a way to pay for me to get there. I lasted a few months before I begged to come home. I missed my parents. I felt lost.

I got back and went to high school as I was always supposed to. I felt different. I looked different. I was different. My goal became figuring out how to be strong enough to leave again. By sophomore year, I was a complete mess. I spent junior and senior year trying to figure out how to fit in and fix my broken pieces, but I still did not know how to really heal.

I engaged in consensual sex during high school. I never really cared about the emotion behind it. To me, at that point, sex was not special. It was scary, but sex could be made to feel good.

Knowing that I had ever felt pleasure doing something I did not want—and knew was wrong—brought intense shame. Now, for some reason, I engaged in certain behaviors and felt shame. What was that? Was I welcoming shame? Did I need it to exist?

I was not used to having a say over my body. I moved through high school and college without caring who did what to my body yet felt so violated when they did it without asking.

And people did things without asking.

And people did things without permission.

Things I should have spoken up about.

I know now that I should have said something. I know now that it was not my fault.

I was sexually assaulted in high school and again in college. Both times I had been drinking. However, I remember protesting. Explicitly.

I remember not wanting to be there. I remember saying no. I remember saying please stop. I remember the tears. Yet, I was somehow made to feel like I allowed the behavior.

I suppose it did not take much to convince me of that, since the belief was established so long before. I sat in disbelief and felt sick to my stomach. I know now what I knew back then, that I had been violated, hurt, and raped. Because I engaged in sex with others before, I was the one that was talked about. I was the slut. I was the one who had rumors thrown around.

I got hurt. I was victimized. Yet, I still subscribed to the belief that it was my fault. Because somehow—once again—I believed that I had allowed it to happen.

Once you have been abused, it is easy to be abused again. Your boundaries are degraded, and you feel it is pointless to re-establish them. You really can feel like that is what is supposed to happen to you. At least, I did.

And there I was yet again. The blame. The fear. The guilt. The shame. I was so wrapped up in being unlovable, undeserving, and unworthy—and at fault.

Once again, I stayed silent.

I always felt like two different people. This bright spirit of a child that had not yet been broken, living in a world where I was broken, trying desperately to fix, to forget, and to repair that brokenness. I would beat myself up about the ways that I managed it. I knew who I was inside. Why was it so hard to reflect that sometimes? How could I convince others of my true worth and value if I could not convince myself? How could I see what it all meant if I had to be silent?

I let people say horrible things about me because I convinced myself it simply did not matter. I sank further into depression when I was home alone, while being as shiny and bright as possible everywhere else. I did not care what the cause was, I just knew the answer was leaving.

It became very simple. I became determined to move away again. Every time I felt sadness, I told myself I could escape.

The reason you achieve? That's how you can leave.

And I did achieve. I was in gymnastics, cheerleading, band, chorus, student council, national honor society, pep club, drama club, and a long list of other wonderful clubs and activities. I was homecoming princess, a scholarship winner, a beauty queen, and a popular girl by most standards.

People often assumed I wanted out because I was superior or thought I was better.

To some, wanting to leave so badly made it seem like I thought I was too good to be there.

It had nothing to do with hating a place. It had everything to do with needing to escape. I just wanted out. *I needed out.*

I wanted to live without the shell I created.

I wanted to be myself.

I wanted to be free.

I have had loving, caring, romantic partners, but I never allowed them to fully see all my broken pieces. I could give myself to other people, but only if they did not ask too many questions or look too deeply. I was skilled at being okay— enough. I covered up the jagged edges by molding myself to the likes and interests of others, while never really defining my own. I could be whatever anyone needed because it was easier than trying to figure out who I was.

I achieved many things in high school. And, on the surface, I had a lot of friends. Surface level was safe.

Deep places unlock scary spaces. Too much closeness brought fear that I would fall apart. I feared I would break my silence and tell the secret. I did not want to deal with the fallout at that point.

I was terrified of what others would say, what they would think of me. And I still wondered if people would believe me. I became an expert at being happy and feeling safe with certain people, and then once someone got too close and asked me too many questions, I would panic.

As I went through college, I broke down even further. I hoped it would be easier, but I was still afraid. College was a LOT of fun, and I was much freer and happier than I had been in years. But I also made many poor decisions out of that space of fear, guilt, and shame.

On top of all that, I missed my parents. Deeply. I was totally unprepared for the loss I felt. Waiting so long to leave all the terrible memories behind made it easy to forget — or dismiss— so many wonderful times. I truly had not realized the sense of safety and security I felt with my parents.

Even now, whenever I feel afraid, I have this deep need and desire to be near them. It is why, when I was at my most vulnerable following the crash, I called my mom. I am so incredibly grateful that I had that option.

During my undergraduate college years, I also inadvertently started my journey to healing. I took my psychology and communication studies classes to heart, working constantly to figure out "what the hell was wrong with me." I remained convinced that I was the problem. I was still unwilling to even consider the fact that something from my past impacted anything in my present.

I went into counseling for other family situations and started my journey with antidepressants and anti-anxiety medication. At one point, I wanted to be a trauma therapist or substance abuse counselor, but the few jobs I had in college in those fields hit too close to home. Even with the mental health support I was receiving, I was separate from my memories. I was so focused on healing myself in one space that I did not acknowledge any other time period existed.

I had so completely divorced myself from those events that I was able to block them out entirely, yet, I still did not fully understand what I was doing. I read about disassociation in my textbooks, but I NEVER would have described myself that way. I was simply not that person. At least, that's what I was trying to convince myself. So, I was depressed sometimes, and also, super anxious, but only because I was absolutely crazy and messed up, remember? Not because of anything external.

I told myself these things over and over, while never telling therapists, doctors, or anyone what would really creep into my mind—the snippets of memories, the panic attacks, the triggers. I numbed out, closed off, and sunk into a deep depression, while somehow still making it through college and appearing happy on the surface.

MESSAGES FOR MOVING FORWARD

Just Let Go

What are you carrying around
that no longer serves your highest purpose?
What is draining your mental energy?
What loop or thought pattern do you need to break?
You do not need to carry around extra weight.
You do not need to take on the emotional burdens of others.
You do not need to live with emotional pain.
But you do need to address
and acknowledge pain, guilt, fear, shame, anger, etc.
Allow yourself to really feel all your feelings.
Seriously! Feel them!
Do not sweep them under the rug or push them aside.
Work through and process that shit.
You can release what's holding you back.
Just. Let. Go.

TRUSTING MY BODY

I have been given a host of diagnoses that have caused various issues and symptoms. Lupus, fibromyalgia, Hashimoto's thyroiditis, Raynaud's syndrome, anemia, gastroparesis, PTSD, depression, anxiety, ADHD. Brain fog. Joint pain. Fevers. Fatigue. Confusion. Vomiting. I cannot even begin to list all the symptoms I have as a result of my autoimmune diseases. Lupus is the ringleader that made everything worse. When I had been feeling so many symptoms for so long, that diagnosis was the piece that made the puzzle come together.

I was diagnosed with Systemic Lupus Erythematosus (SLE) in 2011, after a few years of not feeling well. *Being Whole*, as it relates to lupus, could fill volumes. I hope someday to further discuss. in detail, the ways I have coped— the meds, the challenges I still face—but that journey was its own, and it deserves its own telling. While lupus shook my life and destroyed my identity, it somehow still did not leave me as shattered and splintered as the abuse did. I was afraid when I was sick, but I was not terrorized and panicked by a fear of feeling unsafe. Perhaps this is not the case for everyone, but there is a distinct difference in how I coped and managed these events.

SLE is the main disease with which I have been diagnosed, but it has spawned a host of evil minions that are always at the ready for when I have periods of stress, trauma, or crisis. Symptoms remain available to wreak havoc on my body when it is most vulnerable. They lurk, awaiting any opportunity to render my body weaker through the destruction of my immune system. Lupus, and the host of chronic problems it caused, have ravaged my life in many deep, dark, and evil ways.

At my worst, I thought I was going to die. Lupus forced me to quit my job, drain my retirement accounts, go on disability, and even endure eight months of no food by mouth.

I was utterly broken.

What do you mean I can't work full time?

What do you mean I'm never going to get better?

What do you mean you don't know how to help me?

I fell apart. I had no idea who I was. I did not want to be a sick person, nor did I want to identify as a sick person. I had worked so hard to get to where I was, but I had to try to reconcile who I was now. What if I couldn't be a professor? Who would I be?

Feeling a complete loss of identity after my diagnosis, I actually dug down, did the work, and talked about it. I went to therapy, got on antidepressants again for a while, and integrated my illness into my story. It became part of me. Now, when I introduce myself on the first day of class, I even tell my students. I let them know some of my history and how lupus took me out of the classroom, and how you cannot predict the twists and turns your life will take.

I own that piece of my story and I control my feelings about how it has shaped periods of my life. I did a lot of work to heal those pieces. The journey to finding myself after that diagnosis and through the sickness was the hardest thing I had done up to that point.

Confronting my history of sexual abuse?

For me, that was harder. *Much* harder.

I had never owned it.

Voiced it.

Narrated it.

Felt it.

I could not heal from it because I never allowed it to become part of me.

There are many stories from those time periods. However, because I was very open about that journey, by the time the crash happened, I felt solid in the processing of my illness. I had made my peace with lupus and felt psychologically stable with the impact it had on my life. I was physically in remission and had started working part-time again. I was even on track to return to full-time teaching status. I thought I was *whole*.

Until pieces of lupus came back to life.

On top of the emotional upheaval and state of crisis the crash caused, my fibromyalgia and gastroparesis flared. Symptoms I had easily been managing amped up their game. I had to deal with some frustrating setbacks and work back to a place of better physical health. It took a lot of appointments, caused many tears, and almost destroyed my plan to return to work full-time after years of surviving on disability.

During that time period, my health noticeably suffered. Because my gastroparesis flared, I was vomiting more than ever. I lost weight rapidly because of the vomiting and my inability to digest food. Three months after the crash, I was down to 101.8 lbs.

I called my gastroenterologist many times. The nurses handled my tears with compassion and reassuring words. I was scheduled to get a PICC line and start TPN, but I could not bring myself to keep the appointment.

TPN, by the way, is Total Parenteral Nutrition—nutrition administered through intravenous methods when one's digestive tract is not fully functional. When I am experiencing a flare, what doesn't come out comes up, so to speak. Even during my periods of peak physical health, I can only manage to string together a few days without vomiting. Because of the severity of my gastroparesis, I had experienced the whole "feeding tube" deal before. I had a Mediport in my chest and was "fed" via TPN for eight months in 2013.

I was not going back there.

Not again. Not for something I did not do.

I was PISSED.

I got ANGRY.

I sat in a space where I allowed myself to be mad. I have paid too much for other people's actions. I have also suffered from my own actions and choices. I was not about to let it destroy me this time, even when I felt like I was being ripped in two.

Before anyone cancels a necessary medical procedure, let me just say this: Over the years, I have curated a kick-ass team of amazing physicians. They listen, they advise, and they welcome my input based on our unique and lengthy relational history. It was not always like that, and I will get back to that later—maybe in some other book. But in this space and in this time, I was in really good hands. I promised to keep them updated. They trusted me and knew I would keep up my end of the bargain.

I know when and how to ask for help with my lupus.

You know what that is? A healthy relationship that I built through years of chronic illness. They knew the weight loss and vomiting was a symptom flaring from the crash and were willing to give me a little more time to process and recover my equilibrium. It was important on levels they could not possibly be aware of at that point.

The fact that they trusted me, and I had faith in them, was exactly what I needed. I was actually trying to listen and count on my body. That was, and still is, very significant to me.

Emotional stress and strain are often triggering for autoimmune diseases. I worked through those setbacks intensely, hoping to avoid sliding further backward physically. To say I was a little pissed about all that would be an understatement.

So, I say to you, drunk driver: fuck you.

But also, I hope you have found peace and took a healing journey of your own. I am not mad anymore.

Life needed to crash in on me in order to catch my attention. Enough for me to prioritize putting myself on the right path. There are, of course, other ways that this could happen. Please do not drink and drive to help more people heal.

Regarding my early experiences with lupus: I knew. I knew something was wrong well before my actual diagnosis —when I began having trouble writing. I also struggled with reading and comprehension. Critical thinking skills grew increasingly difficult.

All of this was happening when I was supposed to be publishing and working to achieve tenure as a shiny, newly-minted assistant professor. In retrospect, it had begun years earlier, but because symptoms were inconsistent and relatively mild, I did not realize anything was wrong. I dismissed it all as grad school exhaustion.

When I was sickest, I rarely read. It physically hurt my brain. I would speak notes into my phone, often unable to write or type enough to even maintain a personal journal. Trying to decipher some of my audio texts was quite entertaining. I could barely form complete sentences, much less investigate academic journals and write research papers.

What is my point in bringing up all of that?

Writing this book provoked a lot of fear in me. The ways in which lupus played a role in my healing process also have everything to do with the years before diagnosis. Even though I'd owned that part of my identity and talked about it openly, I realized I needed to let go of much fear to reach the space where I could write my story. Not only because I needed to be ready to share my truth, but also because I had to confront my fear of writing again.

I was flooded with fears—rejection, loss of confidence, diminished brain power, grammar confusion, not feeling smart enough, wondering if I would be successful. I was back to disordered thought patterns, yet again.

These were all things that stopped me from writing a book years ago. I have a great deal more to say about lupus. This brief chapter does not do that journey justice. Through the navigation of my illnesses, I had to really learn, again and again, that I am not in control.

Now I recognize and understand that this plan was made for me. It was all meant to unfold in this way. I did need to heal from the abuse trauma first. I had to come to a place where I can be more trusting in my body and my mind, so that I can help more people. I needed to process on a deeper level so that I could reach out to others and help them.

I was not ready then. It was not time for me to share. Now? There is no going back.

To showcase how deeply I really worked through my lupus struggles, I've included a social media post from October 23, 2013. There are many ways I managed through my lupus diagnosis, but the cognition piece gave me a lot of trouble. This is why I had to readdress it, to go back and heal those wounds more deeply during the process of writing this book.

～

Originally Posted 10/23/13 on Social Media

I did not go and edit this post. Forgive the typos. If it had been on paper it would be damp and stained with tears.

I realize there may be medical advancements, but the reality of right now is that I will live with lupus forever. I will not get cured. I will not receive any life altering procedures or treatments that will make me lupus free. The best-case scenario at this point in time is to minimize organ damage and attempt to prevent further damage from happening.

The story I want to share today is about cognition. This is something that lupus has taken from me that makes me cry and sob whenever I really think about it. Just now, as I write these simple words, the tears are streaming down my face and I'm silently sobbing. I remember parts of how it a started. I was a new assistant professor. I was 30 years old. I had my dream job. I had earned my PhD and had amazing mentors. I had the skills and the knowledge to make a difference. I wanted to write and teach people how communication during difficult times can strengthen relationships. I wanted to do things.

Slowly my ability to do any real critical thinking diminished. I would read journal articles three or four times and I could no longer make sense of them. I would try to write and I couldn't remember how to use a comma. I would sit in my office with my door closed and cry. Worried that I was underperforming at my job. Worried I was going crazy. Worried that something was wrong.

This went on and continued to worsen over the next few years. I know people knew I was going through something. Some probably thought I was just goofing off and not trying to do my research. Others asked me what they could do to help. I went in for tests and tried every treatment, supplement, and therapy under the sun. I went to counseling faithfully (I still do). I searched for answers, but kept coming up empty handed.

The cognition problems spread to more simple things. I began to dread the afternoons when my kids had homework. Alexandra was in 2nd grade at the time. I vividly remember her asking me what 6x4 was. I sat there and I could not come up with the answer. That may not seem like a big deal, but it was a signal of more cognitive decline. I would go on to forget words that I once knew. I would start to put the cereal in the fridge instead of in the pantry. I knew it wasn't right, but I could not tell you where it was supposed to go. This wasn't the result of a rushed existence. I would actively try to recall or remember how things worked or what a sentence structure should look like. I gave myself migraines by agonizing over papers and projects that I should have been able to accomplish. It was terrifying and frustrating all at the same time.

When I was finally diagnosed with lupus I was sent to the neurologist for cognitive exams. She told me I had "normal brain damage for someone with lupus". Normal brain damage. Huh. Who knew that was a thing. I was told that I was lucky I was high functioning before and that most people wouldn't notice my cognitive decline. I wasn't comforted. I noticed. I knew. I felt torn apart. While there were numerous ailments I had to struggle to overcome, this was the thing that devastated me. People would joke that they forgot things all of the time. It angered me. It felt like a slap in the face. This wasn't just forgetting. This was my new life.

Things have improved a bit from the worst point. I don't forget words as often. I still can't read books, because my comprehension is off. My daughter no longer asks for homework help. She said she hates to make me sad. This, of course, makes me even more sad. People tell me all of the time that I should write a book. I think of all of the studies that I wanted to publish and my heart ache. I think of the 10 years I spent in college and I try to tell myself it wasn't a waste.

I'm not bitter. I'm not angry. I work VERY hard, every single day to not wallow in self pity or let negative thoughts overcome me. Sometimes I need to share the day to day struggles. I don't look sick. I don't sound sick. I'm very good at pretending to be ok. Sometimes it all gets to be a little too much and I get sad. Mainly sad because I feel like I let people down. Sad because my kids won't remember the mom they had before I was sick. Each day is a new chance to be a better person. Lupus can't take that away from me.

MESSAGES FOR MOVING FORWARD

Be Grateful and Thankful for Each Step

They are all moving you forward
to where you are supposed to be.
What is this moment trying to teach you?
Growth hurts sometimes.
Especially when it changes relationships
you thought were incredibly deep.
On the other side of that hurt is a beautiful space
where you get to be your most authentic self.
Trust the process...even when it doesn't feel like there is one in place.
Have faith, do the work, and be open to change.

HELP

I used to get anxious asking for help because I felt like I had to take care of things. I felt responsible for anything and everything I was near. Some of that can be attributed to hypervigilance. Control means no uncertainty. It means things are in order. It means things are safe. That has led me to try to be too independent and to resist letting others help when I could really use it. In so many ways, that comes back to trust. I fear people will not be there, but I have to trust enough to let them in.

After I was diagnosed with lupus, I had no choice but to let people help me.

Read that again.

But, letting people help is not the same as asking for help.

I allowed people to help me when they offered multiple times or just did things, but I HATED having to ask anyone. On many occasions, I really should have asked. I am so incredibly lucky that I had people in my life who knew what I needed and were just there. I received a great deal of support and encouragement from more people than I can count. In part, I think it was because I was very open about my journey with illness. I owned that part of my story and refused to let it defeat me. Even though I was not asking for help, people could recognize that it was needed.

I healed, relaxed again, and felt pretty solid.

Then? The car crash happened. And wow. Just...wow.

My control issues and fear of letting people help reached a new level. I felt so scared that I could not even fathom the idea of letting someone help me. The only way out and through was to dive deep, dig in, and get shit done myself.

So, I ghosted. I left life. I abandoned my friends. I deactivated social media. I stopped talking to almost everyone. Even though all those amazingly helpful people were still in my life, I could not let them in. I could not tell anyone what I was really upset about.

It may not have been immediately clear to other people why the crash caused me to close off so much. Because the crash could have been so much worse, most people probably could not understand why it was the trigger that caused me to shut down. To some, it may have seemed like an overreaction. That is one thing about trauma and crisis; you never know how much somebody has already been through. You never know what is going to shake someone to their core. What might seem relatively small to one person may be monumental to another.

Saying I was this upset about the accident seemed so ridiculous, like it was not enough. I felt insecure and unstable. I felt like my reaction was not matching the situation. In part, because my reaction was about so much more than the accident, it was not my classic fight-or-flight pattern. I was in a fight for my life.

I determined that I would conquer this once and for all, but I did not tell anyone what I was doing. Keeping the secret was exhausting. Eventually, I became so tired and overwhelmed that I did the only thing I could think of. I called my mommy.

I picked up the phone. Tears fell, my voice cracked, and I asked my mom to come. I actually uttered the words: "Mom, I need help."

She drove thirteen hours to be there. To hug me and tell me it was everything would be okay. Even though she had no idea why I really needed her. She just knew that if I was asking, it must be really bad.

And it was.

Really. Bad.

My mom ended up coming twice in the span of two months. Staying for a few weeks each time, helping me with everything. Having her with me made everything better because I felt safe. When she left, I felt like I was falling apart again. It was like I was that little girl, finally asking her mommy for help, and not being able to bear when she could not be there.

It was hard.

I could not yet talk to her about the abuse at that point. I just sat in her arms and cried.

I would almost tell her.

Then I would lash out.

Then I would cry some more.

I would get afraid and instead of telling her, taking it out on her was my response. It was my panic. One night, we were on my couch sitting beside each other. I started sobbing and she put her arms around me, and she held me. She told me it would all be all right. She was present. I wanted to tell her so badly in that moment, but fear held me back, once again.

My mom decided to stay for a few weeks because my birthday was approaching and she wanted to celebrate with me. I was excited to have her there because I love birthdays. But this one was different. On the way to work on my 40th birthday, I saw the face of my abuser. I could take you to the exact spot where it happened. Without warning, the image popped into my mind, tears welled, I gasped in horror, and I felt sick. But also? I felt so incredibly relieved.

It was a moment of complete clarity. I knew exactly what I was supposed to be doing. I knew exactly what I had to do. It was time—time to share, time to really put myself out there.

That man will never take another birthday from me again. That man will never again take a moment of my happiness. That man no longer gets to provoke fear in the depths of my soul. That man and those memories are part of my life, but they will not define my life.

My life gets to be defined by all the good things I have done—not by any of the awful things he did. His voice and his words shaped his story. While they may be woven into the tapestry of my life, my voice tells my story.

For months, I knew I was supposed to do something with all of this, but I was unclear as to what that really was. I felt a strong pull to keep going, like this purpose was bigger than me. It was at that point that I decided I had to do something. From that day forward, that I propelled myself deeply into the process of sharing my story.

MESSAGES FOR MOVING FORWARD

You Cannot Stop Hiding Behind Your Pain if You are Unwilling to Admit That it Exists

How do you acknowledge events that have happened in your life?
Do you talk about them?
Do you process your emotions?
For much of my life, I have pushed away pieces
of my identity because I did not want them to be part of me.
I believed I could escape the pain by pretending it did not happen.
I thought that I was strong enough to get through it
without addressing what it had done to me personally.
When we ignore the impact of trauma, crisis, or stressful events,
they have a way of sneaking up on us in other forms.
The pieces can be fragments that reinjure you
over and over in new ways.
Do not be afraid to confront your pain.
Talk to it, break it down, and find ways to let it go.
Do not let the darkness that you are harboring overtake you.

BEING AFRAID

I created patterns out of a need to feel protected.

I held onto a deeply ingrained fear that I could not do things because I was unable to stop something bad from happening to me. For the longest time, I felt that I was incapable of keeping myself safe from further harm. So often, without even realizing it, I created patterns and coping mechanisms that made me feel secure. I became rigid and obsessive about many things. I lost the ability to live in and experience the moment. I was constantly working through every situation. Hyperaware of people's reactions, I was convinced that anything that went wrong was completely my fault.

I allowed limiting or disordered beliefs to become my reality. Many of these beliefs stem from messages I received from my abuser. I allowed his words to be deeply imprinted on my soul. I BELIEVED HIM. His pathology became my truth.

These destructive patterns were ruling my life in ways I did not understand.

I want to tell you about this journey and how pieces of my

life fit back together during this process. The is the healing of deep trauma which stems from childhood sexual abuse. There are other pieces I have healed over the years, but they are not things I revisited in connection with this experience. Although I mention many of these events by name, they do not get a thorough dissection in this space.

While my divorce was transformative, I do not feel that it played a significant role in my healing from abuse, so I chose not to elaborate on it here. There are many themes I overcame during that time period, but those stories belong not only to me but to my children. We will decide when we are ready to share them.

My infertility left me feeling emotional depleted and hopeless, but that pain and those emotions were not associated with this experience. To insert that into this book would be a disservice to my struggle at the time and to all those who have experienced the pain of infertility. I discuss my experiences with illness very briefly as it relates to the themes from my sexual abuse. Again, although this is part of my story, I wanted to focus specifically on rebuilding the things I was not yet vocal about.

Someday, I plan to expand further on all my stories. No piece is more important than another—no piece is less valuable, but at this time, I needed to confront the piece that I was leaving out.

MESSAGES FOR MOVING FORWARD

Feel Your Feelings—Don't Become Them

Feel all the things.
Let anger, sadness, excitement, joy, or sorrow be present.
Do not deny your feelings or where they come from!
Suppressing some or all emotions is not healthy.
When you allow yourself to feel things,
you do not have to become them.
If I get angry, I do not have to let that anger make me an angry person.
Working through your emotions
does not mean placing them on other people.
I can work to express myself in interactions
calmly, kindly, and rationally.
Even when I'm angry.
Do the work. For yourself.
Better relationships will follow.

CLOSING OFF

 he way I survived the abuse was to create a mental escape. I was there, but I wasn't. I got to a point where I felt nothing, and where I could lay there and sing songs in my head and stop feeling his touch. I felt like I was outside of my body, watching the events unfold, but able to stop them from happening.

Imagine feeling like you are separated from what you are experiencing.

Imagine knowing where you are, but not knowing if you are really there.

Imagine wanting to be so far removed from a traumatic or stressful situation that you create a safe space in your mind— a space where you can forget, a space where you are present in body, but absent in mind. A space where you can look someone in the eye, and you do not see them because you have mentally escaped.

Imagine doing this so often that you no longer identify with the stressful events that have really happened. Imagine being so good at detaching that it feels safer than reality.

I am not sure when I started disassociating. I just know it

became easy to shove away pieces of my life like they were not happening or impacting me in any way. I started doing it to not feel the abuse. I kept doing it because it felt safe.

Once the abuse happened, I began to fragment. I no longer felt connected to myself. Those wounds changed my entire existence. I could feel the pain of others, in part, because I was always in pain, and I did not know how to manage that.

I tried to stop feeling. As an empath, that felt damned near impossible. Escaping to a separate space in my mind felt like the easiest alternative to facing the pain. I created a space where I could function, live, and even thrive by detaching myself from the very things that fractured me.

Fear became my constant companion. What if I accidentally divulged the abuse? I struggled to understand and make sense of what was happening so I could rationalize the behavior somehow. I tried my best to internally process what was happening to me, but because I did not speak up, I felt alone and had no idea how to help myself.

I eventually learned to escape my thoughts and feelings about what was going on. I hated my thoughts. I turned inward and learned to disassociate.

So, how do you deal with the shame, guilt, and fear of any stress, crisis, or trauma if you are not going to talk about it?

By acting, repressing, and searching for a way to make the feeling go away?

By distancing yourself from the people you love because you are afraid you will slip and tell them this horrible secret, only to find yourself so isolated and alone because you've shut others out?

Maybe? Perhaps? Can you relate?

Well, that is what I did for a very long time, without even realizing it for the most part.

Most of my friends knew nothing about my abuse. Many of them found out through a social media post when I announced that I was writing this book. I did not always feel safe and close enough to anyone to truly let them in—not because they did anything to deserve that treatment, but because it was another pattern. I tend to let people close enough that they think they know me deeply, yet I close off the deepest parts of my heart.

I spent so much time protecting a secret. I wasted a tremendous amount of mental energy trying to pretend it did not matter. It was exhausting.

Other people often think I am very extroverted. I flit around at parties. I talk to anyone and everyone. I bounce around and probably seem like I want all the attention. I did want attention, but usually at a superficial level. The more ridiculous I was, the less real I had to be.

Did you know that when you talk to everyone about nothing, you do not have to talk to any one person about something deep?

I did not accept the broken pieces. I would not surrender to my past and the abuse. I would not integrate those experiences. They were not part of my identity.

They were not part of my story at that point. I did not necessarily realize it as I negotiated different life stages. I muddled through, got by as best I could, and convinced myself I was fine in many respects. I now realize that my strong need to withdraw and disconnect was a coping mechanism that I have employed most of my life.

Once I identified my patterns, I really had to grieve the loss of many relationships. I saw how, by holding back in many instances, I was hurtful to others. I became incredibly grateful to friends who had been there throughout all of those years. I became increasingly distant to those who I realized were only there during the good periods. I learned a lot from this pattern.

One thing I hated and had to work through was the great sadness I felt when I considered how my abuser changed my relationship with my parents and my siblings. I know we would have had so much more closeness if I had opened up and let them in on these secrets. I cried and I grieved for what I missed. Grieving and acknowledging loss was part of my healing process. I had to allow myself to let go and experience the sadness.

The bright, happy, joyful person who was not afraid is someone I have struggled with my entire life. I know happiness and joy is my true spirit and my true essence, which is why I would get so angry at myself when I allowed the darkness or anxiety or fear to overtake me.

Throughout all stages of my life, I walked through each moment trying desperately to reclaim myself—that person I was meant to be—and that light. I struggle to imagine what my life would have been like had I not been broken. I do not know who I would be. But I did not spend much time searching for those answers about the past. I was more concerned with mere survival.

MESSAGES FOR MOVING FORWARD

Find Your People

You can make connections anywhere.
With people who have might have nothing in common with you
or your station in life.
Be willing to be open and vulnerable.
Show yourself.
Share. Be present.
Watch the world unfold.
Your people are there.
Stop expecting them to be exactly like you.
You are unique.
Find others who showcase their individuality and accept yours.

FIGHT OR FLIGHT

$\mathscr{T}$he urge still comes to run, to flee.

It is not always what you would think. It does not have much to do with actual physical safety. It typically happens when I start to feel emotionally overwhelmed. If I have had a long day without being able to process, when I am overstimulated by the needs of others, or if I have overextended the depths of my emotional energy. In other words, it happens when I am emotionally vulnerable.

Feeling overwhelmed makes me feel weak. It makes me feel like I am not capable of handling things. I am not just talking big stuff either. Normal, routine, daily tasks such as making appointments, filing paperwork, or running errands —things that FILL the life of a chronically ill person—used to amplify the panic within me.

Staying in the same place for too long made me feel uncomfortable and restless. I wondered if I loved being a professor so much because of the constant change. I was always reading new things, changing my lectures, getting new students. I fulfilled my interaction needs through our classroom conversations, which also helped allow me to keep many friends more surface level. It was easy to go with the changes and never focus on what was right there.

I felt most comfortable when seeking and trying new things. Always spinning and moving, I never stayed still long enough to actually have to deal with anything on a deep level. Yet, I desperately wanted things to stay the same. My mind was at war with itself—craving peace while creating chaos.

I struggled to perceive whether a threat was real or not. My fight-or-flight response was always activated, and I expended a tremendous amount of physical and mental energy trying to manage it all. I walked through life exposed and sensitive to everything—so raw, and not knowing how to effectively manage my feelings. Mentally exhausted. Hyper-alert. Frenzied. Neurotic. Overstimulated. Anxious.

Experiencing only surface-level calm, I was sure that everyone else could feel my panic. I internalized this perception and carried it around as part of my identity. I described myself as messy or chaotic or crazy. This gave permission for others to see me in those ways too.

The best thing I accomplished for myself was to learn how to name this and recognize when it happens. For me, it truly does start with a physical response, a fear-based physical reaction. It is very subtle now, starting with a quick flutter in my heart. Then, a small lump forms in my throat. It used to come frequently and catch me off guard. Now, I am much better at recognizing the pattern and stopping it before it becomes overwhelming.

What do I do now when I begin to feel these physical reactions? I tell myself that it is a physical response and I try to process where it stems from. I try to understand what is provoking the feeling.

What have I stopped doing? Freaking out on myself. I stopped telling myself I was crazy, weak, unstable, and hypersensitive. Your inner dialogue is a critical component of healing or being stuck. The way you talk to yourself matters. Communication with yourself and others is an important part of the healing process.

What do I recognize now? I see that enjoying new experiences and accepting change is different than desperately seeking change because you are afraid to stand still, and you feel the need to flee.

I still love change, movement, and new things. That is part of my personality. Running away from things and being afraid is not. It was part of my healing and growth to see the distinction and embrace my authentic self while identifying my maladaptive coping techniques.

MESSAGES FOR MOVING FORWARD

Stop Being Toxic to Yourself

You are not toxic, but the thoughts you have about yourself might be.
Stop being toxic to yourself.
How's your inner dialogue?
Do you build yourself up with positive self-talk?
Or do you erode your self-worth by routinely
allowing negative thought patterns?
Would you let your best friend, significant other,
family member, or coworker talk to you the way you talk to yourself?
What limiting beliefs are you telling yourself?
How are these disordered messages inhibiting your growth?
Tiny thoughts add up to big old patterns.
Your happiness is worth the effort it takes to change these patterns.
Day by day. Step by step.
Moment by moment.
Communicate to yourself with kindness.

Give yourself grace.
Stop being toxic!

FEAR OF FAILURE

I do not know anyone who would call me a failure. I have achieved. I have accomplished. I have succeeded. I have overcome. I have thrived in the face of hardship and adversity. I have risen above more times than I can count.

Yet, because I could not find a way to be peaceful and content, I believed I was a failure.

In part, I did this to myself over the years by not setting strong enough boundaries and taking on too much. I kept trying to be amazing everywhere else because I was failing internally. Then, I would often get so overwhelmed and afraid of failure that I would paralyze myself and regret ever agreeing to do anything.

I did not want my abuser to get the satisfaction of seeing me be unsuccessful. I did not want to fail and prove him right. But beyond that, because I did not feel deserving or worthy, I lived in constant fear of failure.

I had this insane desire to prove myself—not to other people, but to myself. That is why I kept chasing success and achievements. Even when others gave me accolades or told me how great I was or how strong I was, I did not believe it. I simply did not see what they saw. I saw this broken person who desperately wanted to be fixed, to be healed, to be saved.

My fear of failure paralyzed me, preventing me from moving forward. I was unable to consistently be my true authentic self. I have had negative reactions. I have been unstable. I have regretted my choices. As such, I did not feel worthy of success. I always had more work to do and felt I was spinning out trying to get ready to do things instead of just doing them.

My fear of failure was huge. I did not trust in my abilities. Low self-worth was my constant companion. That seed he planted—that it was my fault—grew into an uncontrollable theme in my life. It became embedded in my soul and, when I worked to separate it, I felt like I was ripping myself apart.

I had to learn how to love myself—even when I felt like I had failed.

I had to learn to loosen the expectations and standards I have for myself.

A big piece of being free from this was letting go of my own timeline. I hung on tightly to what I should be and where I thought I would be, judging myself every step of the way. It was necessary to release the pressure of trying to fit into academia again. I had forgotten the part of me that just likes to write for fun. The part that uses slang and tells stories and loves sarcasm and cheesy jokes.

So, disability and illness helped bring me to this place. Thank you for that, lupus. The lupus-induced losses hurt like hell. However, without all of the loss and hurt, I am not sure how I would have found my voice again, and certainly not in such a profound way.

Losing that professor piece of my identity helped me

understand that it was really not my whole identity. I had to learn that trying is not failing.

I want to help people.

I want to teach people.

And, I want to learn from people.

Raise Your Value

How much do you value yourself every day?
Are you making sure your worth is known?
Stop making yourself small.
Stop selling yourself short.
Raise the value you set for yourself and be your number one fan!
I have held myself back numerous times.
I've stopped short of my full potential.
At times, I have failed to even try. I bet you've done it too.
Own it, recognize it, and stop the pattern.
You set your value. Stop putting yourself on sale!
No discounts are needed.
Value yourself. Tell yourself you are worthy.
Find people who value you fully,
people who acknowledge your true worth.

EXPECTATIONS & VALIDATION

I needed to achieve to feel valuable, loved, and safe. I was seeking external validation for something I had not processed internally. Why did I not see that more clearly twenty years ago? That is the benefit of time, I suppose. It has helped me with coping, processing, and healing.

One hurdle I stumbled over time and time again was the enormity of the expectations I set for myself. I did not allow things to be goals or lofty ideas. For me, they became absolute musts. I relentlessly beat myself up when I failed to meet my own rigid expectations.

Any guesses on where that came from?

Any idea on why I clung to my own unattainable expectations?

Deep down, I felt that sense of unworthiness. This is one way it would rear its ugly head. It is not about achieving something. It is about setting the bar so high that I would never reach it. It is about believing I was not worthy of success.

I did not believe I was deserving, and my standard for

success was so unbelievably far out of reach I could never hope to achieve it. Even when I won something or achieved a goal, I knew I had not tried hard enough. If I knew I was never going to reach my expectations, then I reinforced a core belief—I was not worthy of success.

I proved that point over and over.

You know what that is?

Another pattern.

Not only did I fear failure, but I made myself into a failure every day.

One toxic behavior I reveled in? I would constantly compare myself to others and become upset when I perceived I didn't measure up. It was not about their successes or their abilities. It was about not putting myself out there fully. I knew I was always holding back, never reaching my full potential. Even in my achievements, I could have done more, but that would have required all of me. I did not have all of me to give.

There is nothing that I can change about my past. I have released any feelings that if I had been better, stronger, more capable, I could have done something. But then, I thought if I had done more, bad things would not have happened to me or those around me. I thought I did not do enough. I thought I was not enough. For anyone. In anything. Anywhere.

Just so we are clear, that is a disordered thought pattern. That is a whole lot of tightly held guilt and fear. That is not about my ability or my worth.

But I thought it was.

I became overly critical of myself. I became unforgiving when I made mistakes. I let fear control me, and then I would hate that I allowed fear to make me feel weak.

I engaged in a desperate, continual sequence of achieving to negate the things for which I was beating myself up. Yet, every achievement felt empty. Every mistake felt like he won. It was a vicious cycle I repeated until it was no longer a cycle. It was part of me.

I was scared to go back and truly process those years following the abuse. They remain some of my most self-destructive and dark times. My shiny exterior belied what lurked beneath. I now recognize I needed to make all the darkness less scary.

I did have major identity problems. I was always seeking external input and validation because I did not know who I was for so long. Achieving did not feel like an accomplishment. It was a tool to prove myself, but I knew I would never be enough.

If these thoughts feel disorganized, you are understanding the nature of them. It seems to the average person that winning and being enough are synonymous, but they were not to me. They were mutually exclusive.

Can you see how that happens? That flood of emotions? Even years later, even when I felt whole and secure, my blood would pump faster, and I felt the tears coming when I thought of how deeply I believed I was at fault.

I had that shame I continued to confront. Thankfully, it no longer gets to overtake me. It does not get to hide in the shadows. Now that I can feel it, name it, and talk about it, I am in a better place to figure out ways to move through it more completely and fully.

MESSAGES FOR MOVING FORWARD

I Love You

Look in the mirror.
Say it out loud.
You may need to hear it from yourself.

HAPPINESS & PRAISE

J navigated many peaks and valleys over the years. I struggled with mental health. I endured debilitating physical illness, and I experienced great sadness and immeasurable pain. So many crises, traumas, and even what some might call bad luck.

Now, when I combine all my experiences and talk about each bad thing, it almost feels like a work of fiction. And through it all, more than anything, I wanted to be happy. I wanted to integrate all the parts of myself and be whole.

Somehow, I managed to hold onto my positive spirit, much of the time, and I showered the world with glitter. I have been happy. I did not pretend to be happy. I was happy. I am happy. And I was a happy little girl too.

People who knew me probably remember that I loved to sing and dance. That I would talk to anyone. That I loved to make other people happy. I wanted to make others smile and laugh.

Everyone saw that girl.

He saw that girl.

He preyed on my happiness. He told me that is what

everyone loved about me. He said that is what made me so special. It made me want to keep that part of myself so that I would have a chance at being loved. Being outwardly happy was the way to get others to love me.

My brain twisted everything up because he was so convincing. Even when I pushed back, his responses were so expertly crafted. He never wavered. He was evil personified.

"Everyone loves you being happy. It is what makes you special," he would tell me over and over. Yet in the next breath, he would say, "No one will love you because of what *you* have allowed to happen. No one will ever want you."

No wonder I was so confused. There were many mixed messages.

As a child, I internalized the idea that I had to be likeable, because deep down, I was clearly a bad person.

I had to prove him wrong. I wanted everyone to like me. I sought external validation, because I had no internal self-worth. I wanted to be loved, but I also wanted to hide.

His words mattered more than my own feelings. I trusted his words. I did not trust my feelings. There were too many years of psychological manipulation, too many years of not understanding what was happening, too many years of displacing myself to the point where I did not know who I was or what I felt.

Even though I wanted the approval and acceptance of others, I did not know what to do with it. I was uncomfortable having any real attention focused on me, all the while striving for that attention so I could prove I was lovable. I was going back and forth between the person I knew I was and the person I felt I had to be. I felt like I was splitting myself further in trying to make sense of the turmoil and emotional chaos he created.

Certain memories stuck out to me, even if I was unsure

what to do with them. These were benign occurrences that should not in any way be remarkable, but they cut back to the themes of needing validation but being unable to accept it

For example, one day in gymnastics practice I performed a warm-up pass, and one of my teammates complimented me. She expressed this in a kind and supportive tone. I disparaged my efforts, and she and another teammate asked me why I could never accept a compliment. They questioned why I would not simply say thank you.

That moment is forever burned in my memory. Those girls were supportive. They pointed out something so obvious. This was something that should not have been a defining moment, but it STILL makes my stomach churn a bit when I remember how I felt then. I felt like I had been punched in the stomach. I felt like my skin had been peeled off and I was standing there with my heart open and exposed.

I knew exactly why I could not accept a compliment. I knew exactly why I tried to downplay that attention, while also desperately wanting the approval.

That terrible man.

His words haunting me.

Ripping my soul and fracturing me into pieces.

Out of nowhere.

In my safe space.

School. Gymnastics. Those were the places where I was not supposed to think about any of that. It was in the past.

But it wasn't.

It was right there. Standing on the red gymnastic mats in a leotard, I lived his words. I heard him tell me I was beautiful and how everyone would want me; then, I listened as he doubled back and twisted it so that no one would ever love me because I was used. He complimented me every time he saw me; then he threatened me.

And so, compliments were not always positive to me. I wanted them. Praise felt good, but they also made me uncomfortable. I did not always trust the motive.

Compliments were not genuine praise; they were emotional manipulation. I did not believe I was deserving of compliments. That is how deeply those themes of being unworthy and unlovable were embedded in my psyche. Simply accepting a compliment is something I had to learn. It sounds so silly, but I had to train myself to simply say thank you instead of explaining why I was undeserving.

I had to tell that fractured part of me to stop taking over. I had to change my inner dialogue.

I am worthy.

I am valuable.

I am awesome.

I truly believe those things now. Praise me all you want and watch me bask in it!

I am thankful to my fellow gymnasts from all those years ago in that routine gymnastics practice. It may have taken me years to process, but that one trigger forced me to realize something more was wrong. That piece—the unlovable piece—can still be incredibly sharp. It cuts swiftly and deeply.

MESSAGES FOR MOVING FORWARD

Pick Up Your Pieces
They Make You Whole

I have been broken many times.
I have felt shattered beyond repair.
Yet, somehow, I've routinely picked up the pieces and started over.
Each time, wondering how I would go forward.
Every time, coming out stronger than before.
I look back at different times and think about how healed I felt.
Then, I see where I am now, and I realize how much further I am.
That does not mean I was failing before.
It means I have continued to grow in my healing.
I've continued to work.
I've rebuilt and made myself whole,
but I have to keep moving forward.
I am continually evolving into who I am supposed to be.
Your growth is unlimited.

Your power lies within.
Pick up your pieces.
Make yourself whole.

AWARENESS

"*A*re you afraid of the dark?"

One of my doctors asked me this simple question when I was forty years old. Restful sleep has eluded me for many years. I remember being a child and being afraid someone would come into my room. I knew every escape route in my house. I knew where the guns were, and I had a detailed plan for saving everyone in my family depending on where the intruder entered. I know it seems so obvious, but I had not even considered how my need to feel safe impacted my sleep as an adult. I did not make the connection between my need for escape routes and my ability to achieve restful sleep. I never realized that my patterns were woven so deeply that they continued to have physical manifestations.

I have a fear of being stuck in one place. I have a fear of not moving forward. Probably because I have been in a situation where I was stuck, held down, and unable to move. After discussing that with my doctor, I continued to unravel ways the trauma impacted me on a subconscious level.

One obvious example is that I need a means of escape. I like to have multiple ways to leave any one place.

A few months after the crash, I decided to move. I had been living in a large two-story house that I had occupied with my kids and my ex-husband during our marriage. After the divorce, the kids and I stayed, but I often felt overwhelmed with the huge task of caring for the house. I also grew increasingly panicked at the idea that there was only one exit out of that neighborhood.

I felt trapped. I walked into that house, where all our bedrooms were upstairs, and I felt scared. How could I keep everyone safe there? I knew I had to simplify my life as much as possible.

I wanted a smaller house that was more manageable, both financially and from an upkeep standpoint. I felt like I had a chance to start over in all ways, including choosing a new space for my kids and myself. Feeling safe in my home was self-care.

My hypervigilance has manifested itself in many different ways. It made sense when actual danger was present. But I also had to revisit and dissect routines I have had for years. There are little rituals and preferences that I do not really notice until something happens, and they are not in order.

I confronted some of these situations and discovered I was doing them most when I felt unsafe. As I was thinking through things, I would feel that slight fear response. That is one way I knew I was striking a chord.

Although I was healing and working through my fears, there was an element of safety I had trouble shaking. So, one big factor I looked at when buying our new house? Multiple exits. How many ways could I leave if I needed to? How many potential exits were there out of the neighborhood? What alternate routes could I take if I felt stuck—or trapped? It was not really about the abuse, but it was about the larger patterns I had created. These rituals helped me feel safe.

Another significant thing that would surface is that I would always immediately jump to the worst conclusion about everything. Hypervigilance turned into criticism of myself and hyper-awareness of everything. If you do not text me back, I assume I did something wrong. Hypervigilance can completely destroy how you interact in relationships. I wish I had known what I was doing day after day, year after year.

I have gotten much better about relaxing some of my strict and rigid ways. I even ride with friends to events instead of taking my own car. That is a big one. Because having my own car goes back to having my own escape, which means I can bolt the minute I feel I need to. This used to happen frequently out of nowhere. I now try to make a conscious effort to tell at least one person when I have to leave a situation.

When I finally broke these patterns, I got really good at setting better boundaries for myself. I got clearer on my relational needs and what I actually wanted. I told my friends and family members when I felt unsafe, what triggered me, and asked for their help. Being able to voice and articulate when you feel unsafe is an incredibly monumental step in healing.

Having people who make you feel safe even when you are at your worst? That is the best thing anyone has ever done for me. I was lucky. I had people who tried hard for me and did that over and over, even when I did not know why I was afraid or what I was afraid of.

MESSAGES FOR MOVING FORWARD

Small Moments Create Big Patterns

What are you doing for yourself?
How are you working on your own growth?
Think about this in terms of relationships,
work life, and even self-care.
Small moments create big patterns.
What are you building? What routines are you creating?
Are they healthy?
Do your daily activities help you reach your goals?
If you are stuck, step back and ask
how you might be contributing to that feeling.
What small manageable steps can you take today?
Can you do those again tomorrow?
And the next day?
Tiny movements forward will add up over time.
Small moments create big patterns.

COPING WITH THE BROKENNESS

*A*s we have established, I do not always utilize the healthiest coping mechanisms.

I have covered up the broken pieces with everything possible. Drugs, alcohol, shopping, superficial friends, sex, school, work, volunteering, reality television—even random hobbies.

Any and all things possible.

Truly processing all my pieces has taken many years and a variety of methods. It bothered me that I would not always finish things. I would turn away and not confront them, because I did not want to face fears and be in pain. This theme has extended to so many things across various contexts. I've numbed out in various ways and kept myself very busy with work, motherhood, volunteering, going out, and whatever else I could in a feeble attempt to make it all go away.

Let's just say this: I have come a very long way.

Thank you to those who made it through the bad years. Depending on who you talk to, they are very different years.

How have I made myself unlovable over the years? Let me count the ways.

I took my feelings—the fear, the guilt, the shame—and internalized them. I assessed every situation from that space without even realizing I was doing so. I have self-sabotaged and made enough bad choices that it was easy to keep believing what he told me all those years ago. No one would love me because of what I had allowed to happen. This message resonated, playing on repeat.

Looking back, I realize I desperately sought to fill that empty space, and nothing—

absolutely nothing—was ever going to be enough. The broken pieces, with their jagged edges, belonged in that empty space. By pushing them aside and not processing them, I was leaving a massive, empty hole.

I wanted to have my mug shot be the photo heading for this chapter, but I do not exactly own a high-resolution file of that beautiful photo. So, instead, I will share the relevance it has to this chapter of my life.

Over the years, I medicated myself in many ways. My lowest point of self-medication came at a time when I appeared to be doing fairly well on the surface. I had just returned to work part-time, which was actually harder on my body than I acknowledged to anyone. I had been divorced less than a year and was trying to piece things together for the kids. I was in more pain from the increased activity and daily wear and tear of life.

Drugs, my own prescription drugs, ultimately became my worst enemy. They were also an easy excuse. I really did feel pain, so taking painkillers and muscle relaxers was reasonable. I had the prescriptions. It was a routine.

I had also started taking a new antidepressant. Wine, muscle relaxants, and pain meds were often the only way I was able to get some sleep at night. It was not restful sleep, but it was still sleep and an escape from the pain.

It was all legal, until it wasn't. I had not realized that even tiny bits of alcohol were making me black out because of my mixture. After numbing out, I was usually at home in a deeply medicated slumber, but one day too many margaritas consumed alongside my prescription cocktail caught up with me. I got arrested for public intoxication and spent the night on a concrete floor, freezing and questioning my life choices.

I do not remember much from that night leading up to jail. I do remember being in jail. My phone had died so I was unable to look up any numbers. So, I called the one I knew best. My mom's.

I do not recommend calling your mom from jail. Actually, let me back up, I do not recommend going to jail.

You know what I do not do anymore? Take muscle relaxers and pain pills and drink to go to sleep. Chastise me all you want. I know it says right on the warning label of the medication not to mix with alcohol. I am here to tell you that people will do a lot to cover up pain.

I have numbed myself more ways than I would like to admit. During the bad lupus years and especially when I was trying to go back to work, I was in a lot of intense pain. Sleeping was damn near impossible because every single cell of my being was on fire. Every joint in my body throbbed and each bone weighed a ton.

Do I think mixing pain meds and muscle relaxers and alcohol is the answer? No, it is stupid. Did I care? No. I did not care until I went to jail. And I did not remember anything. I did not care until I realized that it was altering my moods. I did not care because I was escaping.

After that night, I swore off the pain meds and the muscle relaxants, and I got off that particular antidepressant. I also stopped drinking for quite a while. I was so deeply ashamed. I felt like there was no recovery from my bad choices. I believed I was destined to live in that space.

I had to work really hard at that point. I started owning up to my behavior and I stopped going out as a means of escape. I stopped attempting to numb things. I was still experiencing physical pain, but I did not want to take any meds.

Once I stopped taking meds, I realized how altered I was when I was on them. They made me angry and spacey. Looking back, I cannot believe I did not realize how OUT of it I was. I am now one of those people who is thankful to have spent a night in jail.

There are no excuses for my behavior. Please do not read this explanation as such. I have had plenty of other nights of bad choices. This one produced a lot of shame. This night forced me to stop and wake up a little. It was another sign that should have pushed me to confront old feelings, but I kept going back to the mental state of safety that came from filling space. Memories were popping up more, but I still was not willing to believe that any of it mattered.

Not everything you feel is the result of something from childhood. Nor is everything you feel something that must be traced back to a particular moment or pattern. If you have changes in your needs or you are not sure why you feel something, it can be helpful to go back and do a little digging to see if you can figure out where that is coming from and what needs to be addressed.

MESSAGES FOR MOVING FORWARD

Stop Sabotaging Yourself

How are you sabotaging yourself?
How are you limiting your growth?
Something was holding me back,
and I had the power to change it.
I was not very nice to myself.
I allowed the negative self-talk to override everything.
Do you let fear and doubt creep into your mind?
Do you stop yourself before you start?
Do you tell yourself you can't do something?
How can you change those thought patterns?
What small manageable steps can you take
to create change in your own life?
In what ways are you holding yourself back?
Stop trying to break yourself further to make it all go away.
Integrate those negative experiences.

Bring them into your story.
Make yourself whole.
Put the pieces together in a way that
showcases your individual beauty.

SILENCING MYSELF

*I*f I would have said something, I could have altered the outcome.

It is a terrible feeling to know the course of your life was altered so deeply because you did not use your own voice. It brings shame.

Deep shame, along with regret.

I did not speak up. I allowed myself to break into pieces, and I completely walled off the abuse like it never happened. Yet, it happened over and over. I never spoke up about what he did to me.

I did not do enough then, so I never felt like I was doing enough in the present.

How long will I keep trying to fill that space?

I even stumbled over that fear while writing this book. Too much time had lapsed. I had lost some of my writing ability. I didn't know how to share this story. Maybe it didn't even matter.

What about the people who did not know it had happened? I did not tell when it was happening. Why would I talk about it now? Who would care? What could really be done? What was even the point?

I was scared to speak my own truth and use my own voice, all while advocating and teaching others to use theirs. As you can imagination, this felt like next level hypocrisy. And it was a total mindfuck.

The trauma made me even more sensitive to issues I perceive to be unequal or unfair. I know the sexual abuse was not fair and it was dead wrong, but I also had to forgive myself for not standing up for myself or countless others through a variety of unfair situations. It makes sense that I have this deep need within me for things to be fair, this finely-tuned sense of justice. I really hate that anyone would be in a terrible situation for something they did not do and they did nothing to cause. I hate the fact that anyone has to suffer for something out of their control and for something that was done to them by others. That is why I needed to help others. I became an advocate, an activist, and an ally.

I felt strong. Capable. Helpful. I LOVED helping others.

But I also felt like a fraud. Why was I so good at helping others and so incapable of fixing myself?

It finally hit me. The crises I repeatedly faced were, in effect, wake-up calls for my own healing, but I was not listening. You know what's really interesting? How I distanced myself from the thoughts of my own abuse while immersing myself in the care of others.

I teach classes where abuse is a prevalent topic. I lead discussions where people disclose their own abusive situations. In addition to teaching, I volunteer to help educate others about the signs and symptoms of abuse. Yet, I did not even consider many of my own lived experiences. I did not stop and let any of that connect to my own fragmented past.

I had a disconnect between helping people and helping myself. Helping people and teaching is when I feel alive, vibrant, and truly at peace. It is me being guided by something greater than myself. Helping myself made me feel crazy and unstable, like I was so incredibly messed up, but I did not know why.

I have pages filled with the things I have beat myself up with over the years. If an award existed for negative self-talk, I would have been a major contender. So, during the healing process, I thought about my silence. I knew I wanted to speak up. Yet I knew I could not begin to reclaim my voice until I healed in earnest.

By remaining silent, we allow our inner thoughts and beliefs to speak all the lies we have believed about ourselves over the years. By speaking up, we can silence that inner dialogue. I had to process. I could not speak on a larger platform about this until I had healed. It would have been irresponsible and damaging, to myself, and to others.

I needed to wait, so I embraced silence for a little while longer. I was so done being scared that I went inward, tuning almost everything and everybody out so I could reclaim my life. I do not necessarily prescribe this method to anyone else, nor do I think that works for everyone.

Given my responsibilities and the demands on my time, it was the only way. I had been through trauma therapy before. I have had years of counseling. I knew this time I had to do things differently.

I did continue to check-in with my medical team and healing practitioners. I do not advocate isolating yourself or not seeking help. I did seek help—lots, in fact—but it was of paramount importance to protect my space. I needed to go inward and process, at this point, rather than processing, yet again, with others.

MESSAGES FOR MOVING FORWARD

Your Voice Matters

Through the power of our own communication,
we have the unique ability to change each
and every moment of our lives.
Talk to yourself with kindness.
Show others compassion.
Observe. Learn.
Grow.

REBUILDING MYSELF

You ou know what I remember most about all the difficult times? What really sticks with me? Even in the very darkest days, the light burned inside me. It propelled me forward. That strength—that voice—that is what I remember. Telling me to stop, sleep, or just let go.

I got through the worst times by believing I could. Even when I did not want to. Even when I was downright exhausted. Even when I said I was done.

When I started putting myself out there a little more, I realized the myriad of ways fear was still embedded in my life. I had to stop letting fear hold me back. I am still that vibrant happy little girl. She is NOT dead. She is NOT gone. She has guided me and lived inside me, helping me survive, never leaving me, showing me that I am loved and protected.

To deepen my healing, I had to face the fear. Ultimately, my fear had much to teach me. I had to embrace my power and recognize that I am not helpless. Through my healing, I decided to use my voice to help others.

When I released more fear, I became brave enough to

move into a space in my life I had only dreamed was possible. I gained confidence in my voice. I spoke louder and more clearly. It was not scary any longer, but it took me a very long time to find the strength to confront my fears.

Over the years, my coping mechanisms became my patterns and shielded me from harm. My walls and my armor protected me and kept me safe, like maladaptive patterns can. I simply neglected to see how I was allowing these fragments of trauma to reinjure me repeatedly.

For me, *Being Whole* was about acknowledging those broken pieces. Broken pieces have sharp edges. They might splinter and leave fragments, all of which cause wounds. These wounds had to be identified and treated, so that I could finally heal.

Being Whole is knowing your value. Not just day to day or because you look good, being whole means knowing it from deep within and working through dark times because you honor the light inside, even if it is only a flicker. Sometimes, that comes easily. Other times, the darkness can be all encompassing.

Finally, forgive yourself. Find the light again.

MESSAGES FOR MOVING FORWARD

Reevaluate, Refresh, Reframe

Reevaluate, refresh, and reframe your mindset.
Some days it would be easier to be pissy and pop off to people all day.
At times, I really feel like just wallowing in self-pity.
Being negative gets you nowhere.
You did not go through everything you have in life
to sit and be miserable!
You have not worked this hard to sabotage yourself.
Not on my watch.
Move forward, people!
But hoooooooow? I can't!
Go on, pile on the excuses! Give them to me! Let's do this!
I am never going to just say simplify your life.
I think it's complete bullshit.
I've got stuff to do, bills to pay, and a million dreams to chase.
I've said it before--find what works for you and your lifestyle.
I have to be practical.

I have limits with my time, money, and energy levels.
I do not have an endless supply of cash to throw
at my happiness and self-care.
So, I do positive self-talk, turn to my faith,
complete extensive journaling, do lots of meditation,
or dial up my safe people and meltdown.
All those things are FREE!
What's your excuse now?
I know positive self-talk sounds cheesy.
My teenage son tells me every day how stupid it is.
I'll tell you what I tell him. Try it!
Prove me wrong.
Report back and complain to me about
all the ways that positive self-talk has ruined your life.
I will be waiting to discuss your findings.
P.S. I will bring lots of citations to this meeting to help prove my point.
Many of you live in your head anyway.
You might as well make it a nice place.

COMMITMENT TO MYSELF

I was very much on edge throughout this process of deep healing. I found myself at a place where I was just done. I needed it to be over. I asked doctors and therapists several times if I could just take meds and STOP.

I am a firm believer in mental health care. I have taken all sorts of anti-anxiety and anti-depression medications over the years. It is NOT a negative thing, and certainly not a sign of weakness, but it is also NOT what I needed at the time. I had to keep up with the actual processing too.

I know my patterns, remember? I recognized if I asked for meds or tried to numb my reaction to the realization, I would have, in essence, been doing exactly what I had done so many times over the years. It was crucial for me to keep going back to the memories to uncover my patterns and my disordered thinking

I was honestly a little worried that, if I had one more crisis or emotional breakdown, it would be too much for my kids to handle. Between lupus, disability, and divorce, they had already shown such resiliency. I did not want to challenge their resources once again. In reality, my kids were solid. Their coping skills and patterns have been routine conversations in our household. I have been determined to make them healthy in ways I was not, which is once again why I had to do this for me. And, for them.

Of course, it was rough for my kids to bear witness, once again, to my deep pain and sadness. It was hard for them to want to help and not know how. Crises, trauma, mental illness, health issues, and other life challenges do not exist in a vacuum. They impact those around us in profound ways. Family structures, friendships, workplace relationships, job stability—the list of how our challenges and struggles cut through life seems almost infinite.

I am grateful that my kids and I are very close. We talked through everything, and I was open with them about my needs and my goals. Even with all my own shit, I am their rock. I am their stability. I do not get to quit on them.

Single mom life means a lot of emotional labor. It was HARD to take that space for myself, but because of our closeness and relational history, my kids knew that I would not waiver. They knew I would not be broken, even as I felt like I crumbled. They believe in me and trust me more than I often managed to believe and trust in myself. Ultimately, I needed to commit to healing and view myself through their eyes. It required a lot of work to see myself realistically.

I was working hard, putting in several hours each morning before anyone else was up, so I could work in solitude. I drank my coffee, meditated, prayed, journaled, practiced yoga, grounded, cleared, and cleansed. Anything and everything I believed was positive and helpful to my recovery and healing. Anything I did not fit into my morning routine came after work, dinner, activities, bonding, and everything else that happens in the life of a busy family.

It was not any one thing that healed me. It was about the

process of taking time for myself. I wrote pieces of my story. I cried. I processed. And I healed.

I wrote a bit about the benefits of narrative therapy way back in my dissertation and have been talking about it in classrooms for years. I did expect to use it for myself again and again, but I found comfort in the practice. In some way all of this helped me find and reclaim my voice. It felt amazing, but if I'm being honest, it was an exhausting time.

There were days when I felt like I could not physically or emotionally do more work—times where I wanted to give up for good—but there is no way I could. You see, doing the work wasn't actually scary to me at all. In many ways, over the years, with all my different crises and traumas, healing work actually became another coping mechanism. In the process of my healing, I also analyzed my quest for healing over the years.

I obsessed about new treatments, books, and therapies. Every time I experienced even a small setback, I decided I was completely broken and needed to plunge into the next cure to heal myself. Every time I messed up, got too emotional, or cried—I was a failure. I neither loved, nor valued, myself enough to extend the grace I provided so readily to many others.

Eventually, I broke that pattern too.

Revisiting the memories and processing the pain of my sexual abuse and psychological manipulation is the hardest thing I have ever done. Ultimately, I needed to figure out who I was before the abuse. It was necessary to learn how to integrate what I had been hiding and let the darkness be revealed so that each of my pieces could fuse together. I had to give voice to the pain so I could defeat the fear.

I was finally ready to:

Feel my feelings fully.

To confront my mistakes.

Learn my lessons.

And *grow*.

My abuser stole so much from me. And I've come to terms with the fact that I will never get back what he took from me. I will never be quite the person I once was. *How could I?* The profound loss and sadness I felt was immeasurable. Putting the pieces together and really feeling and fully acknowledging the depth of my loss felt like too heavy a burden at times. Much of the time. The sadness and grief threatened to overwhelm my emotional resources.

When people are hurting, they want quick answers and strategies that will help them heal. I wish I could say it was easy. And here's what helped. Unfortunately, I do not have that. For me, it was a combination of tools, techniques, and healing modalities, and I was open to trying different things —or anything—that possessed healing potential for me. This was a piece I had not been able to get to before; my usual methods needed revision.

Do not be afraid to explore the things that work for you. There is no one prescription for healing.

MESSAGES FOR MOVING FORWARD

You are Worth the Work

You are worth the work it takes to stay physically, mentally,
emotionally, creatively, and spiritually healthy.
Invest your energy wisely!
Time is our most precious resource;
how much are you giving back to yourself?
Are you doing the work to keep yourself healthy?
What practices do you employ to keep yourself centered and grounded?
You deserve to start the day in a calm and peaceful way.
I do not have a prescription for healing,
but what I do have is many years of trial and error to share.
Find what works for you, in your life, at this point in time.
Make it a habit and applaud yourself for
taking time to keep yourself strong.

SEEING MYSELF

*L*et's just say that my romantic life does not look quite the way I ever imagined it would. A divorce never figured prominently in my life plan. Following my divorce, my next significant romantic relationship was with the boyfriend who was with us in the crash. And, when I *thought* I was almost done with the book, our relationship ended. That sad ending became a new beginning and, as difficult as it was, it propelled me toward further growth and positive change.

Although we are no longer together, I still consider our story to be one of great love. He was there through times of great significance in my healing story. We had various challenges and neither of us bear the full responsibility for the breakup. In the end, it was the healthiest relational ending I have ever had.

I know we truly had great love for one another in a certain time and space. I can honestly say that I am proud of how I handled things. We both did the best we could with where we were at the time.

Before you feel sad for me, let me say this.

I am good.

He is good.

Things are going well for me.

Things are going well for him.

We are both where we are supposed to be.

I am healthy, happy, and I know I will have the best relationship of my life sometime in the future. But that is what I understand now. This is about what I felt then. This is about how I was feeling unsettled in our relationship and knew it had to change. This is about me figuring out my needs.

I knew it was right for us to be done, but I still loved him. That is one thing that made the breakup so difficult. I learned a huge life lesson. Your needs come before your feelings.

I failed to articulate my own needs—in part, because I did not know what they were. The crash made me realize so much about myself, my needs, and what I wanted for the future. I had to really think about what I needed, wanted, and was willing to change. In so many ways, that had nothing to do with him.

He was the same. But I was different. And I came to know myself in deeper and more profound ways.

As I began to process and heal in earnest, I could feel the closeness that we had achieved slipping away. Feeling it, fearing it, but also not understanding why, I had no clarity or sense of why I was doing it. It was not about sex. It was not about my feelings for him, yet slowly I felt the walls emerging. This feeling was all too familiar, and I knew it was happening. I could not demo that wall, even though I wanted to so badly. I was unable to see that the more vulnerable I became, the less I could be open and emotionally available in my relationship.

My need for stability skyrocketed in the months following

the crash. I didn't just want security; I *needed* it—emotional, physical, and financial security. Feeling safe was paramount. I did not want to manage everything on my own.

I needed a partner on every level. Yet, so many of the facets of our lives were things I was in control of—things I had always managed, things I had always done. In part because of legality and logistics. I no longer wanted all that weight. Even in the face of some of those struggles, we forged ahead. I desperately wanted to believe we were unshakeable, but we had been shaken—deeply and painfully —from the drunk driving crash.

My panic from that was omnipresent. My distress led me to confront more fear but not before it robbed us of our spontaneity and our simple pleasures—like taking long drives —and it stole my ability to let go in the moment. That was our space and it was gone.

I had been working so hard at healing. Things *should* have been back to normal. I was done with processing. Right? Surely, I was, yet I was unsettled. Again.

I had to figure it out.

I was frantic to know—and understand—why I was feeling this way.

When I dove headfirst into my post-crash healing, I failed to recognize how I was turning away from my boyfriend. I wanted to be near him. Always. I wanted him so close. But, when he was close, I felt the need to be alone. I did not want to talk to him about what I was uncovering. I did not want to share the details with him.

I felt scared.

Of what, though?

I had no clue.

It gnawed at me. Feelings of insecurity and anxiousness would freak me out.

It was making me angry. It was making me sad. WHAT ELSE WAS LEFT? I had literally revisited every memory and healed my emotional reactions to them. I had talked to my family about everything. I had processed my other memories more deeply, my job was going great, my kids were happy, and I was slowly reentering my social life and allowing people back in.

I realize now that while I was able to articulate when I was mad or frustrated, I struggled to identify the source of these emotions. I struggled to explain why, all of a sudden, things that were once fine with me were no longer acceptable —why now I needed more, on every level. I was angry at myself for wanting more and upset with him for not providing what I needed.

From his perspective, it probably felt like I had changed all the rules without warning. I could not adequately explain myself and my feelings. I blamed the accident and mentioned the book, but still, I chose not to fully explain and enlighten him to what was really going on with me. I was simply not ready.

I had come so far and felt so whole that I did not understand in any way what I had left to heal. It came in waves—feeling fully healed and, then, so very low. I felt confused by the instability I felt in our relationship.

There I was. My book was mostly written, but I struggled to piece it all together and take the next steps. I even joked that there better not be another piece to fix. I felt so close, but I did not know why I was having trouble moving through this block. I felt desperate to uncover what was holding me back.

And then the answer came.

Swiftly, cleanly, and painfully.

As soon as I had it, I felt free, yet so deeply wounded. I

broke through the last bit of scar tissue. Before I got there, I told him our relationship was over. I told him I was done. He packed, moved out, and I woke up.

I did not realize until after we broke up what my core issue comprised. I was still hanging onto a big broken piece. I did not see what it was doing to me. It is SO incredibly obvious when I talk about it and describe things now.

Again, remember how deeply my patterns were ingrained. I was 12 when the abuse stopped, and I was 40 before I really understood all those years that were stolen from me. So, let's return to the scene of the crime. Remember how my abuser told me no one would love me? Recall how he told me that, because I might have gained any small amount of pleasure from him touching me, I was to blame?

He told me no one could possibly love me for what *I* had done. I believed it and internalized the blame for his predatory, criminal actions and psychological torture. For years his words cut through my soul and poisoned my thoughts. I have spent my whole life wanting to be loved, but also pushing it away. I realized that, in part, even with my boyfriend:

I did not believe I was deserving of love.

I did not believe I was a good person who anyone could truly love.

I understood the unlovable theme, but I had not yet truly internalized what it meant and how deeply rooted it was to the very core of my being. I had not examined it in terms of my current relationship. Truth is, my heart, and my ability to fully love and be loved, were severely compromised by the emotional and psychological torture visited upon me by my abuser.

In many ways, I suppose you could say I sabotaged the relationship, but we were also growing in different ways, in different spaces. I already mentioned that in my quest for healing, I turned inward. It felt like survival, like I was working to save my life. He was there, but I was no longer "seeing" him fully or completely engaged in the relationship.

Entrenched in my own darkness and my own broken pieces, I did not have space for friends, nor did I not have space for him. Still, while I recognized this, it hurt—deeply. I loved him. Although I was more open, free, and true to myself and my needs than in previous relationships, I was still not fully myself.

After we broke up, I was happier than I had ever been. He did not hold me back, but I had been holding myself back. The aftermath of the breakup, although immensely painful, served to remind me of my own strength and resiliency. Still, it was a confusing time of profound peace and happiness mixed with the sadness of the loss.

MESSAGES FOR MOVING FORWARD

Your Needs Come Before Your Feelings

Know your needs.
Your feelings will follow.
It doesn't matter how good someone makes you feel.
If your needs are not met, it will be hard to be happy.
Period.
People want to be happy and satisfied in relationships,
but rarely take time to establish what that means for them.
What does your happy look like?
We all desire different amounts of control, affection, inclusion, etc.
What do you need to feel like you belong?
To feel safe? To feel loved?
Do your relationships meet those needs? Or are you chasing a feeling?
What are your deal-breakers?
For real! Go deep. What do you require for happiness?
If you want emotional depth,
why are you settling for partners who are incapable of providing that?

If you want someone who is a good listener,
why are you still with the person who never pays attention to you?
Once you get clear on your needs,
you may realize there are people you need
to let go of in all areas of your life.
That's ok!
You can honor and thank them for the space they held.
And then?
Go forward.
Even when it hurts and is sad.
Especially when it hurts and is sad!
You are defining what you need.
Sometimes just articulating those needs,
or even figuring out what they are, is a big challenge.

LOVING MYSELF

I plunged deep into the one off-limits area I had never been able to navigate. With great resolve, I confronted the mental trauma and emotional manipulation that accompanied the sexual abuse. I was integrating all the memories and allowing myself to feel that pain so I could finally let it go. In retrospect, that anguish had seeped out in so many ways over decades without me realizing or acknowledging the toxic source. Not surprisingly, experiencing the abuse and deeply processing those memories really shook me.

I failed to recognize the myriad of ways the abuse changed me, fragmented me, and altered my perceptions. I had always blamed myself for every disordered thought I ever had. Once I confronted the core issues and patterns, I felt some peace, but the unrest and feelings of being stuck continued to reinjure me. I truly believed, after all those years, that no one could ever love me. I believed I was not worthy of love. I believed that because of what *I* had done I would never be lovable. Of course, I regretted that I did not recognize this sooner, but I felt great relief to be finally to this healing place.

No one wants to feel pain, and I was no exception. But I knew that further growth required me to walk down this path. I still sometimes wish it could have been different, but it was apparently what needed to happen for me to really see how I needed to heal. I was cut to the core in a way I have never experienced. It is why and how I got to my deepest scar tissue imaginable.

I let my boyfriend closer than I have ever let anyone. Even though I built walls, I still let him into a space that I had never opened for anyone else. I showed him pieces of me that no one else knew. In so many ways, I wanted him to stay. I wanted someone to prove to me I was lovable, but first I had to believe it fully for myself.

Again, although I was sad, I was also free from that piece of fear that had been imprinted on my heart. While it felt amazing, I felt the stark emptiness of my walls finally being gone. The sadness came because I thought he would be there when they fell. He was supposed to get to bask in the glory of how I finally found peace. Instead, significant growth came through this space.

Throughout this time, I realized more about myself and my needs. I achieved clarity about my desires for my future. I recognized that my wants and needs are valid. I finally understood I deserve for my needs to be fulfilled. My needs do not make me selfish.

I wanted a partnership where I was no longer required to be the strong one all the time, but where I can let my guard down. I learned again, that I was—and am—strong enough on my own, for myself. I do not need to sacrifice my healing and my wholeness. For the first time in my life, I fully made myself my first priority.

Our relationship was a lot more than either of us expected or were looking for when it started. It evolved into something so beautiful but in many ways, I do not know that either of us was equipped for what it all would entail.

It was the most magically healing time for me. I thrived. I felt joy, I felt like I was and am the best version of myself. Every day I blossomed further. It was when I remembered myself and got to leap and live in this space of awe and wonder again—not because anyone was absent—but because I was present.

MESSAGES FOR MOVING FORWARD

Wanting Someone to be Right for You
Does Not Make Them Right for You

Choose relationships that meet your needs.
Look at your friendships, romantic partners,
workplace connections, and your family members.
Refuse to settle.
You are deserving of happiness.

EMERGING

A tremendous weight lifted when I disclosed my abuse to others and began to talk about it freely. But, a raw, open, and vulnerable space revealed itself. So much of my daily existence and even the personality I showed to the world was part of bandaging for the gaping wounds I possessed. So much of my energy and effort were dedicated to surviving and healing.

What was I supposed to do with this emotional space now?

All I knew was working to keep myself safe at all costs. Those walls I had carefully constructed and maintained for safety and security were beginning to crumble. So, seriously, what now? The walls were crumbling, but they were, essentially, what held me up for so many years, and I had to figure out how to live without them. What would that look like? Who was I now? Putting plans into action, forging new paths, and living without the walls was continual work for me.

I felt really raw and incredibly exposed, and also a bit empty and scared. Figuring out how to live in this new space was a critical task. I had to figure out how to live in the new space. I had to learn to fill the space in healthy ways. I started working out again. I kept up my healing practices and became fiercely protective of my time for myself.

I realized I had the chance to rebuild, grow, and change—to really create the life I wanted. I allowed myself to cultivate new relationships and release those that were no longer healthy. I spent time growing. I observed things with new possibility.

I decided to start speaking to groups. I decided to grow outside of academia. And, I decided to reach for my new dreams.

MESSAGES FOR MOVING FORWARD

Be the Person You are Today
Regardless of the Mistakes You Made Yesterday

We all make mistakes.
You cannot change what happened yesterday,
but you can move forward into a new space today.
To what limiting beliefs do you subscribe?
Does fear hold you back?
Do you worry about the perception of others?
Shift your mindset.
Move forward and release those negative patterns.
Acknowledge the feelings,
process them, and set them free.
Start fresh every day!
Your mistakes do not define you.
Learn from them, grow, and heal.

BEING FREE

*F*reeing myself from old patterns was no easy task. There were many negative thought processes I had to work through. I needed to stop myself from engaging in cyclical behavior. I had to change by myself and for myself.

There are many things that helped my healing, and there are many challenges I still confront; however, the difference now is that I do not feel instant panic every day, and anxiety is no longer a state of being for me any longer. The mental chains that confined me for years have slipped away. I will continue to be a work in progress. My mind feels freer, and I experience greater clarity, because I put time and effort into my own happiness.

I am proud that I invested this effort in myself. It is no longer optional for me. And, most importantly, I know I am worthy of it.

I do not always get to choose how my day unfolds, but I do get to choose how I respond. Rewiring the patterns of self-blame, doubt, fear, guilt, and shame has been my greatest challenge.

You do not have to be solid all the time to be healthy. You don't have to smile every moment to have happiness and contentment. Sometimes, we just need that one small thing that can keep our spirits alive.

I have helped many students figure their lives out but, for reasons I've described, could only do it for myself on a surface-level. I did not love and value myself enough to think I deserved the deep emotional healing that I helped others find.

I still work on this every day. Yes, even on those amazing days where I feel invincible. Just like I need to put effort to maintain my physical health, I accept that I will always need to work on my emotional health. The steadfast dedication to my own emotional health has helped me rebound in moments when I feel like I may spiral. Even when we are positive and can cheer others along, being our own advocates can feel exhausting. I do not always treat myself the way I should. I push. I make myself cry. I verbally abuse myself and I lapse into negative self-talk in weak moments.

Then I stop.

I STOP.

I realize what I am doing, forgive myself, and analyze my thought patterns and what led me to that place. That, right there, is the best thing I can do for myself every single day.

I didn't used to stop.

I used to let those feelings and thoughts consume me.

I used to start the cycle all over again.

I've been working on breaking this cycle for years. It is not easy for me, or for most people who have disordered thinking. It doesn't mean you are abnormal. It does not mean you are broken. It does not mean you can't overcome. Cut yourself some freaking slack!

You are worth the work it can take to remain emotionally

healthy. You are worthy of deep love and understanding. You are valuable. You are loved.

MESSAGES FOR MOVING FORWARD

Be Happy Now

What criteria are you setting for yourself?
Do you say you'll be happier or calmer or more peaceful
once you hit the next milestone?
Do you say you're only going to be less
stressed once you get a vacation?
Do you bank on happiness to appear once something is finished?
Stop feeding yourself that bullshit.
Be happy now.
Even in times of stress.
Especially in times of stress!
That is when you need to remind yourself how far you've come.
Be proud of all you have done.
Thank yourself for being strong enough to get to this place.
You get to decide.
You can be happy in this moment.

You can look at your life and find the positive pieces.
You can say, yep, I'm super stressed, but I've got this.
Find some happiness in your day to day life instead of waiting for
magical moments to appear.

EMOTIONAL

*O*ne mistake I often made?

I assumed all people are damaged and that they would understand my pain without judgement. People LOVE to judge the emotions of others. They also love to assert how they would act in situations they have never faced or can't even possible truly understand.

I won't lie. Having my emotions judged, looked down upon, and casually dismissed has been one of the most difficult things for me. Always emotionally sensitive and deep, I process internally, but I still like to hear it out loud. I have to talk through things with myself. Sometimes that is enough, other times I seek external sources to hear me out.

Here is the deal; by the time I process externally, I usually have it all figured out. By the time I talk to someone else about something, I have been thinking about it on my own, often obsessively, for a very long time. Usually, I already know exactly what I am going to do. Other people can be taken aback by how quickly I move forward after I finally talk about a problem, concern, or future plan. Most of the time I do not need or want advice, but I want a dialogue where we look at things more deeply or where I can share what I've uncovered.

This has been my process for getting through things my entire life. It was hard to be told it was wrong or unbecoming or something I needed to fix.

I have to let the tears and anger flow and then I can begin to process and understand.

Over the years, the abuse got stuffed down more and more until I could no longer contain it. I felt unstable and wondered if I were bipolar. I would process the thoughts and feelings and then be fine until the next time. Sometimes this was rapid-fire, sometimes it was much slower and more deliberate.

As you can possibly imagine, I lost a lot of people I viewed as friends during that time. And, I further shut out those who in no way deserved it. I stopped trusting that this was my process and began to fear that I was just going crazy. I do understand and acknowledge that there is a time and a place, and sometimes we must check ourselves in relationship to our surroundings. HOWEVER, I also think being more accepting of a wider range of emotions and encouraging emotional processing would promote greater emotional health and, ultimately, make the world a better place.

I know a lot of people who think I am still ruled by my emotions. But you know what? I will no longer apologize for any of my feelings or emotions. And, yes, I absolutely believe I need to release and channel them in healthy ways, but there are a lot of people in this world. It is perfectly acceptable if my vibe is not yours, or if a different way of healing and processing works better for you or someone you know. It is not about being right or wrong, it is also about acknowledging that there are different ways to do things. For me, part of being free was and is speaking my truth. Part of it is truly allowing myself to feel the emotions and then set them free. I believe that part of my purpose is encouraging and supporting others who are traveling a similar path.

Despite everything I have been through, all the ups and downs and large and small bumps in the road, I feel more positively-centered and spiritually-grounded in the present and for my future. I now possess a peace that I only remember feeling when I was very young. And I am finally reunited with that little girl who did not know brokenness. I will not let her go.

MESSAGES FOR MOVING FORWARD

*Your Opinion of Yourself Matters
More than the Perception of Others*

*You cannot control what others think.
Do not waste your precious energy trying to change other people!
You are so much more than others perceive.
Do not let the opinions of others matter more than yours!*

CONTINUING

*T*here will continue to be times when I feel broken. And, there will still be things I have to confront. I fully embrace that now. It was necessary to release my expectations of healing. I will have moments of sadness and stress. I will get overwhelmed and exhausted. There are times when I feel like I cannot think any more thoughts or talk to anyone for a while. Some days, even looking at social media feels like more stimulation than I can manage. But you know what? Now I can recognize my triggers of emotional exhaustion or overstimulation. Because I am not also in fight-or-flight mode with heightened awareness, my lows are nowhere near as low as they once were, and I find myself recovering more quickly each time. I trust that I am OK, and I recognize that I heal more and more each day.

Take the small steps daily, even if they are the same steps. Take them again.

Talk, write, whatever. Process how you process. Then DO it and go forward.

Small moments create big patterns.

When I get scared, I sometimes ask myself, "Do you want

this thought creating your future? Is this real? Or is it a negative belief? Is it a disordered thought?"

That is how we break patterns. We recognize them, name them, and work through them. It only makes sense that we keep doing this to maintain our healthier patterns. Healing is a process. It is continual. I cannot judge myself when patterns arise. I can applaud myself for recognizing them and do the steps again. The only person stopping me is myself. Prioritize your healing and treat that time in your life as life-saving medication.

That also means I do the work to keep healing. See how it comes back to that? So, for example, even as I finished this book, there are some things I needed to work on.

One example? I used to think I was undeserving of success. That is a disordered and sad thought. Of course, I am deserving of success! And so are you! It's not pie—there is enough success to go around and we can all have some. I know this, and, yet, I did not value myself enough to believe I really got to have success. When I have a bad day, that low self-worth can still creep in. My triggers are things I will work on for the rest of my life. My themes of feeling unlovable and unworthy relate back to those triggers of fear, guilt, shame, failure. My fears show me areas that need more work.

To be clear, I do not walk around constantly thinking negative thoughts, and I make plenty of choices that have nothing to do with the patterns. Sometimes, people are so eager to label others that they do not see the whole person. I am—and you are—incredibly complex. Life is complicated and emotions can feel messy.

I do now completely believe and know I am worthy, deserving, lovable, and valuable. I know deep down that I am a kind and caring person who only wants good things for the world. I genuinely believe that most people are doing the best they can with where they are at the time.

On any given day, at any given moment, you might be involved in someone else's patterns. That can be a very hard space to travel. Being emotionally healthy does not mean you have to heal everyone else. Being healed means you stop giving all your emotional energy to others and take care of yourself. It means you know the boundaries of what you can and should do.

You cannot save space for everyone. It means that you are willing to walk away from relationships or situations if they are bad for you, even if someone else says they need you. Your needs come first. That is being truly free. It is often easier to fill time with other things or other people's problems than to reflect and fix our own.

My healing process has not been pretty. I know I have lashed out. There are times I have been mean. There are times I have closed myself off. There are times I have emotionally flooded. I've been, well, all the emotions. Knowing that, I created new goals. My new expectation of myself is that I try to be better. In each moment, in each day. Not in a perfectionistic way but, rather, in a healthy and centered way. The main thing I do is try again. I do recognize my patterns when they arise. Instead of beating myself up, I actually tell myself, "Yes, you could have done things differently, and here is how you could approach that in the future." And then, I thank myself for the process.

MESSAGES FOR MOVING FORWARD

You are the Person You Need to Be Today

Most of us are carving out a future the best we can.
Sometimes, that involves trying to figure out
who we want to be in the future.
Other times, we beat ourselves up for who we were in the past.
You may not be the person you want to be tomorrow,
but you are exactly who you need to be today.
I mess up. I say things I shouldn't.
I let things bother me that I can't control.
I am not proud of every decision I have made.
Each day is filled with new opportunities for growth and development.
If you had already reached your end goal,
how stagnant would the rest of your life become?
Each change we experience helps move us forward.
Don't just go through each day.
GROW through each day

Everything you have been through has led you to this moment.
Do not waste it!
You are the person you need to be today.

FORGIVENESS

ou know who was hardest to forgive?

MYSELF.

I was.

The hardest.

To forgive.

Yes, ME.

I simply could not forgive myself.

I have so many wonderful memories of childhood—so much laughter, so much joy. I had a large extended family full of cousins and second cousins and friends who felt like family. It was difficult for me to understand how I could love my childhood when it was filled with so much pain.

I was 37-years-old before I thought about how the sexual abuse had damaged my life.

I was 39-years-old before I said it out loud to a doctor and asked for help.

I was 40-years-old before I sat my family down and looked them in the eye to discuss the events that took place all those years ago.

Writing this book and sharing my story has been part of my healing journey in a deep and profound way.

This was not only about healing from abuse. This was just as much about forgiving myself—for the bad choices, for not knowing, for not making connections, for ruined relationships, failed friendships, anxiety, pain, and depression.

Forgiving myself is being free. I do it daily. There are lots of layers from all those years and many disordered thought patterns. I catch them and call myself out on them. I refuse to beat myself up when they happen. Instead I recognize it, try to see where it comes from, and let it go.

Year after year, I have had to put out fire after fire, crisis after crisis, never feeling like I had recovered from one before another would start. About half of what has happened to me is in this book. There are other stories that aren't mine to tell yet or that have to wait for their own time.

After I forgave myself, it dawned on me that much of my being afraid should have been called being strong—because I was strong. I WAS strong to withstand what I endured, just as I am strong today. I do not want this to be my whole story. It feels like a smaller piece now, yet its magnitude cannot be ignored or minimized.

I do not think we can blame everything on our past. I had to go back to my past to recognize where some of my choices and patterns originated, but I still made a lot of choices on my own. This book scratches the surface of what I have experienced and does not fully discuss or even look at some instances. These are my big pieces relating to childhood trauma. The ones I needed to fully understand. Everything else is still falling into place. I am, and will forever be, a work in progress. Through the forgiveness of myself, I am finding wholeness. From release of my secrets, I am finding freedom.

MESSAGES FOR MOVING FORWARD

Honor Your Own Limits
Respect Your Own Boundaries

If you don't maintain your boundaries,
you show others they are up for negotiation.
Remember, you get to decide what you can handle.
I work on this in small ways each day.
Usually, I know I've created a boundary violation
when I feel a little twinge of ickiness.
Like when I volunteer for something after I said I wouldn't
or when I agree to go somewhere even though I have plans.
That twinge, gut reaction, feeling, intuition, whatever you call it,
is a signal that I am not honoring my personal choices or limits.
I have always struggled with the reactions of others.
I did not want anyone to be upset.
I would often change my boundary to accommodate their needs
all while ignoring my own.
Doing so would lead to a lot of negative self-talk and

put me in a frenzied panic.
Enough!
Stop trying to be all things for all people.
Be what you need first.
Your needs have value.
Honor your limits and set some boundaries!
It will likely upset people.
It may cause some tension.
That's all right. Don't waiver.
This is not about anyone else.
It is about what you can manage given your constraints.
Pay attention to the reactions you receive.
Thank people who respect your space and honor your limits.

REESTABLISHING BOUNDARIES

*B*oundaries are not the same as walls.

Taking time for yourself is not the same as isolating.

Drawing inward, when needed, is not the same as disassociation.

Now that we have the basics, let's talk about how I adjusted my boundary setting in the face of my healing. This was a lot of hard work, especially when I was deep into my own healing. My being there for others—which I very much wanted to do—could be very overwhelming. That self-imposed isolation was necessary. I needed more time by myself. If I kept giving it to other people, I was never going to heal.

Because I like to help others, I have usually put their needs before my own. I have said yes and taken on things when I really needed to say no or was just maxed out. I would get angry and resentful when I had nothing left for myself.

I recognize now that I do not always have space for people emotionally. I get overwhelmed if I have not had proper time by myself to process, meditate, and reflect. I am now much better at both recognizing when I need to create this space for myself and at finding and securing time in my schedule and without wavering. There are times when this is much easier for me and other times when I struggle to set the needed boundary. Again, it is all a process.

When I reemerged socially, I really tried to protect the boundaries I had established during my time off the grid. This took some trial and error. After healing, I jumped into a few relationships too quickly because I was so excited about how happy I was. I thought I could just spread that happiness constantly to whoever was in need.

I quickly realized that I have worked too hard to give away my energy and not have my needs fulfilled. The beautiful thing is that I enjoy stronger, more stable, and happier relationships because of saying no. I learned what time I must fiercely protect, and I do not give it up for anyone. Paddle boarding, writing, meditating, listening to music, and just being—those things helped me heal. This is important and bears repeating.

I am going to keep healing every day, and the things that make you feel better should not be pushed aside once you feel better. That is so important. Make them a pattern. Healthy patterns can and should be a thing. Become skilled at protecting that space and keeping your healing practices alive.

It used to take becoming frantic for me to remember why I needed to set boundaries in the first place. I would grow angry at myself or at others for expecting too much, but if I willing gave them space, can I really be mad they took it? I knew I needed to get clearer on my needs and limits. I know exactly what I need now, but I am the first to admit that I do not always get it when I need or want it. If I do not get up early or build in a space for myself somewhere in my day, everyone suffers.

This is especially necessary when I am teaching. I throw myself into my work and give my all to my students, willingly investing every ounce of emotional energy I have into my classes. I now understand that if I do not make time and space for myself, I will go home and be short with my children. I will be overwhelmed and tense and need to recharge a bit.

To help with this, I no longer use my drive time to catch up on phone calls. What used to be a time to catch up is now a time to catch my breath, so I can collect my thoughts and prepare for the rest of my night. I also make a point to talk very openly with my kids about where I am emotionally. Some days, that means I walk in the house and say "Hi, I love you. Can't wait to hear about your day, but first I need a second to just be."

I may take that time while I am cooking dinner. Or I may seriously go in the bathroom and have a good releasing cry. The how does not really matter. It is the fact that I do it. My kids are older now and that does help. I am fully aware how different it is to have young children who are so dependent and teenagers who are more independent.

When my kids were younger, I went straight from work to daycare, home, cooking, cleaning, homework, and bedtime. I was so incredibly overwhelmed, I found it almost impossible to protect my space. I was too tired to stay up late, and if I woke up early, so did one of the kids. I'm not saying any of this is easy. Especially if you do not live near family and cannot afford to hire help, it is extraordinarily hard. So, whether you are a parent and/or have a life of many other demands, you really do have to find what is going to work in your life to give yourself the space to do the work and heal.

In an effort to help others open up, I became very emotionally available to people. I allowed them to take all of my energy. I spent a lot of years holding space for other people without reserving ample space for myself.

Now I realize I do not have a lot to give away. I have a tight schedule. I have quiet time built-in because it is essential to my well-being. If I bend and give that away, I end up suffering. And so do my kids.

Knowing how to allow others in while maintaining boundaries is a life skill that I did not possess for many years. I tended to do one or the other. Abuse badly degrades our natural boundaries, and part of healing is reconstructing them in a balanced, healthy, and functional way. And, most importantly, it is a vital means of self-protection.

Standing by my boundaries, even by simply protecting my quiet time, does not make me mean or bitchy. It means I know my emotional limits and how to set boundaries. I am proud of that. I have taught others to do it for years, and I am finally actually doing it for myself in a way that honors my needs.

MESSAGES FOR MOVING FORWARD

Don't Change Your Boundary
Because of Someone Else's Reaction

One of my favorite things to teach about is boundaries.
For the longest time, I was convinced I did
not know how to set boundaries.
However, I realized I do set boundaries,
but I do not always follow through or keep them solid.
Often, it comes down to setting them clearly
and knowing for yourself why you want and need the boundary.
If another person reacts poorly or doesn't respond well,
I can go back to my why.
If I change my why, I am showing the other person
that I did not value my boundary enough to stand by what I stated.
If I break the boundary, I did not stick up for my belief.
And guess what?
I do not get to be mad at someone else for shifting my own beliefs.

Know your boundaries and communicate them clearly—
then stick by them,
regardless of the reactions you may receive.

FINDING PEACE

I once lived life walking around in a state of near panic. We have established my fear that things are either completely great or they aren't. I was operating on a 0 to 10 scale where the only options were 0 or 10. After I broke down some walls, I realized I did not have a good sense of how to handle things that were just OK. It made me uncomfortable. I had learned to live best in extremes.

I used to wonder who I would be without the trauma of abuse and the physical and emotional stress of serious, life-threatening illness. This mystery is one that I am sure many individuals ponder and of course can never fully know. I know now that I am exactly where I am supposed to be. By accepting this, I learned to quiet my mind a bit more and find some inner peace.

My faith and spirituality have changed a lot over the years. I grew up attending Sunday school and singing in the church choir. I said my prayers every single night, and I always asking for the same thing. I listed every member of my family and asked God to keep us all safe, and I ended every prayer with, "I love you God. I love you Jesus. Please keep us all safe."

As a young girl, I prayed feverishly every night for God to keep me safe. As the abuse continued, I began to fear my prayers went unheard and would continue to go unanswered. I felt angry at God and, for a time, stopped believing in much of anything. I spent time trying to find a church where I fit in, rather than reconciling what provoked my anger in the first place. It was necessary for me to redefine what my faith meant.

My spirituality now encompasses the belief that there are many forms of church and numerous ways to worship. Not everyone has the same faith journey, belief system or practice. Part of being free is allowing myself the freedom and flexibility to exercise and practice my spirituality and religiosity in new ways. I rediscovered meditation, prayer, and self-reflection.

Eventually, I redefined my spirituality and reconnected with that piece of myself. I am spiritually fulfilled because I no longer use it as a tool to search for myself. My spirituality feeds my soul and renews my spirit. Through these practices, I nourish myself.

I do not believe the ways you practice your spirituality have to be rigid or confined, but I have always been more gracious and open for others on multiple levels, while placing restraints on myself. Being open in my practice has freed me on many levels. I am not interested in telling people there is one path to do this. I had to find what works best for me, and I honor that others have to do the same.

Once I achieved greater healing and did more work, I stopped worrying about unraveling every memory. Healing is a journey too. It took many years to build patterns and it may take that long to undo them.

I know I am not alone. I did not see that piece for a while. I was still so angry without even realizing it. The universe expands before me with all its magic and possibility.

So, here is what I tell myself and what I would say to you:

Your growth is unlimited.
You are on the right path.
Everything has led you to this moment.

I truly believe these statements. I require positive affirmation, and I provide that to myself now that I believe these words. These words were prompts for myself, and I encourage you to feel these things in any area you may need a reminder:

It was not my fault.
I did my best.
I am safe.
I am loved.

Now that the previously elusive peace resides deep in my heart, I experience a renewed sense of purpose and passion to use my voice to help others heal and grow. Now, I do feel peace in my heart, even when chaos reigns in my outer world. Piecing together the most broken parts of myself brought balance to my existence. They no longer had to cry out and demand to be heard.

Despite the tremendous sorrow, deep wounds, incredible grief, and unbearable pain, I have also been blessed by unspeakable joy, impenetrable love, endless gratitude, and fulfilling peace. What stands between you and your own sense of peace?

We all have experiences that have made us feel less than whole.

We have all felt tired, scared, and broken.

Remember, your pieces make you whole.

We can all work to recognize that people are made up of a bunch of pieces. We do not know or see all those pieces. Before we make judgments about others, we can remember they may be wounded. When we see ourselves as whole and act accordingly, others begin to reflect that back to us.

I am finally experiencing what being free is really all about. Now, I am free to write in a way that soothes me. I am free to teach in a way that is authentic, and I live with a sense of peace that calms my mind. There are moments when I am not thinking about anything. For years, I had no idea that was even possible. So many of my disordered thoughts—the things I was communicating to myself—were deeply embedded in my subconscious, draining my energy and never allowing me to fully rest.

Once we can accept ourselves as broken but beautifully whole, we begin to extend grace to others and their brokenness does not define them. I fervently believe we are all in this together. I have allowed fear and low self-worth to hold me back, but collective healing helps everyone and, ultimately, makes the world a healthier place. So, I will continue to use my voice to help others heal.

MESSAGES FOR MOVING FORWARD

Your Influence Goes Beyond Your Followers

Your influence goes beyond your followers.
Also?
Your worth is not measured by the number of followers you have.
Please reread that until it sinks in.
I know the game because I've played it too.
Other people look like they have the best life.
You see everyone's happiest moments,
you wonder why they get so many likes,
or you wish you were included in the fun you see online.
You want to be noticed.
You want to matter.
No one likes to admit that social media bothers them,
yet it is something that is routinely
mentioned in my classes and workshops.
I hear stories of sadness and depression.
I completely understand the hurt feelings and

the lack of self-worth that can come from those comparisons.
We are inundated by images and messages
that can make us feel like we are less than.
Scrolling your feed and watching stories can leave you
feeling like your own story is not that amazing.
If social media makes you feel bad...take a break.
You can also unfollow, mute, or unfriend people.
You are in control of what you see,
who follows you, and who you follow.
Do you know what is more awesome than increasing followers?
Reducing negative feelings.
You are an influencer every single day.
You may not have thousands of followers,
but you have kind words, a smile, and compassion to spare.
Share those things with the world.

GETTING CLOSE

I can't say it enough: Breaking free from my own patterns was a difficult process. I keep practicing and working on breaking every pattern a little more each day. I am being more intentional. I am, somehow, feeling even more deeply.

I teach about close relationships, but I sometimes struggle to keep them. I am light years from where I was, but even now I have a very difficult time feeling emotions associated with closeness unless I am with someone in person. I want to be able to really hear you, see you, and listen to the tone of your voice. That makes me feel connected and safe. If I have managed to stay close to you without seeing you often, it is practically a miracle.

If you met me and knew me during my really broken periods, you probably fall into one of two camps: those who saw me and recognized that I was going through something, or those who thought I was crazy and are now left wondering how I could possibly write a book about healing when I have fallen apart so much.

Prior to reaching this point, I walked the line of knowing how relationships should be—

of being able to teach about how to have healthy relationships, but never really and truly feeling worthy and deserving of having them for myself. Of course, this caused more than a little self-doubt and imposter syndrome. Who was I to be telling others how to help themselves, if I could not help myself?

I found it impossible to establish boundaries. Fear was my near constant companion. I did not honor my own needs or feel I deserved to even have them. It was so much easier to give to others, help others, and be there for them than it was to keep working on myself. I felt stuck in a perpetual loop of needing to heal myself yet helping others more.

As I have said before, in order to really heal, I pulled back from a lot of good relationships and friends. The amount of work I had to do on myself was overwhelming. Brimming with my own feelings and emotions made it difficult to be fully present for anyone else.

I still have moments—sometimes minutes, sometimes days—where I inadvertently return to the feelings of being unlovable and unworthy, and the belief that my feelings are not valid. There are days when shame, guilt, and fear bubble to the surface. There are times when I let my old patterns take the reins. The beauty in all of it is that I now recognize it much more quickly. I still spiral, I still fall, but I get back up a little more quickly each time.

I have learned to recognize my patterns. I reach out to people. I apologize. And then, I BELIEVE THAT THEY FORGIVE ME, I FORGIVE MYSELF, AND I STOP BEATING MYSELF UP. That's a huge accomplishment for me.

It is impossible to protect everyone, and we do not always make perfect choices, but we can acknowledge our needs and express them to our relational partners to help each other gain understanding. We can learn how to share and process our feelings and experiences while not letting ourselves become trapped by our traumas or weighed down by our difficult experiences.

MESSAGES FOR MOVING FORWARD

Choose People that Fill Your Soul
Instead of People That Hurt Your Heart

Who engages you?
Who enriches your life?
Who makes you feel inspired, empowered, and appreciated?
You are not for everyone.
You've heard that, right?
But guess what else?
Not everyone is for you.
Make good choices!
Healthy relationships feed your soul and fill your heart.

RELATIONAL GROWTH

*W*e always have the power to change our relationships. It is also possible, if not probable, that profound healing and self-discovery will significantly alter our relationships in not so predictable ways. When we are doing the hard work of healing, it is also possible that our closest relationships may struggle to accept the new person we are becoming.

When we rise above our circumstances and pain and our partner or family member or friend cannot or will not meet us there, we must respect ourselves enough to either accept what we cannot change or even choose to remove ourselves from the situation. This is a piece that can be a huge challenge. After we establish healthy boundary-setting, we must be willing to walk away from the people and the situations that don't work with these new, healthy boundaries. The alternative is to accept these situations or alter our boundaries so that we don't grow bitter and resentful.

Separating the emotions from the moments can be challenging. It is important to feel the feelings while not allowing the feelings to take over. We must acknowledge the hurt and the loss, as well as the pain and the anger, but it is important to remove ourselves from situations that continue to provoke all those emotions.

As the years passed and I went through some of the other challenges I have mentioned in previous chapters, I learned how to be more open, and this led to healthier relationships. But I can honestly say that I had never revealed my true self to many people until I healed from the abuse.

My fear and anxiety began to dissipate when I finally started talking about the abuse, Still, if I am overwhelmed or tired or procrastinating or anything, fear is typically my go-to emotional response. Whenever I begin to draw inward now, I ask myself where the fear is coming from and make sure I am being honest with my emotions. My goal is to differentiate and check for drawing inward for emotional space versus avoidance. The former is healthy, while the latter indicates to me a need to figure out what's going on and deal with it.

I highly value time for myself. I enjoy solitude. I like people, and I enjoy my social life, but I need to have my own space to recharge and clear my mind. My isolation is not always a sign of disassociation. Now, I realize the difference and recognize my triggers.

Coping mechanisms serve an important purpose: they keep us safe. But do we need such elaborate safety routines in every situation? For me, learning to trust myself and let that guard down was hard. Letting people in was difficult. And allowing others to see the true me? Scary as hell.

Those coping mechanisms feel safe, which is exactly what I needed as an abuse survivor. Also, as someone who was dealing with a serious illness, I kept repeating patterns. On some level, I thought I was keeping myself safe.

Being vulnerable is not just about what we say. It is about

being open in other ways. It is letting your guard down and making yourself vulnerable and emotionally available and then building healthy relationships based on that openness. Once I dug into my "trauma stuff" a little more, I had this realization one day: spending time with others also makes me feel safe and secure in the relationship. For me, that reinforces that I am loved.

Simply put, being whole takes a lot of work. It is hard, scary and, sometimes, it feels lonely. There is also an amazing gift that comes with the healing: the relationships you DO allow in your life will be richer and more fulfilling. This creates a new radiance and resiliency that you are giving yourself regardless of whatever relationship you are working on.

What fuels me going forward? I want a healthy loving relationship with myself and with my family. I want closeness. I know I will experience that in a deeper, more meaningful way now and I am so excited for each day of renewed growth and authentic energy that radiates from my being.

Through the healing process, I realized I was better at friendships than I had previously believed. When I stopped thinking I was bad at friendship, I looked around and saw the friends I'd had for years. Those who knew enough of me and saw the up and downs and stayed anyway. Those who, after I'd healed, did not throw old patterns in my face. Those who had seen me as whole all along.

So, after a little trial and error, even while finishing this book, I solidified myself once again. My friendships and close relationships do need to be built on mutual trust and respect. I get to choose. I will no longer choose relationships based on proximity, activity, or obligation.

I do need friends, but if I have friends, I want my needs to be met. And I would hope that we would be in a reciprocal relationship where we discuss our feelings, our needs, our desires, and our values. I want deep connection. I no longer have energy to give to those who want something else.

The thing is, not everyone will acknowledge and appreciate your growth. Some people will try to contain you in spaces that you have long outgrown. Some individuals may sabotage you or hold you back due to their own insecurities or issues. Sometimes, the people who have the biggest problems with your new boundaries are the people who benefit from you not having any in the first place. It is interesting to me how I see people so differently now. I am less tolerant and less willing to accept all blame, yet I am more open and excited for the depths of relationships I have.

I also had to shift my focus. I really did not see how good some of my relationships were because I was constantly focusing on those that did not make me happy. So, you know what I did? I ended relationships where I felt unhappy, stressed, anxious, or devalued.

That sounds obvious, doesn't it? But we tend not do that. Instead, we often stay in relationships out of fear or routine.

I realized my needs were not being met, and that impacted my connection. That did not make anyone bad, nor did any of them deserve to be villainized or mischaracterized. We simply had different needs and goals. Though I do think about those individuals from time to time, I recognize how much happier I am now that I am building more authentic relationships.

There are a lot of lost years, with a lot of people, where I was walking around broken into so many pieces. Repairing things felt insurmountable on many levels. Shutting down and closing people out is still one of my greatest struggles, but I finally found people that know the difference between me needing to reflect and my patterns of disassociation, people I feel safe to open up around, to melt down to, and just be still with if that's what I need.

I also still go to therapy and keep up practices so that I am not overtaxing or burdening others with my own needs. One person should not be your everything. It is too much to ask someone to take on all your emotional struggles, so I did what I tell my students to do—I created a deep bench. I have a variety of people I turn to for different types of needs.

It took me three decades to get to a place where I was no longer hiding and being scared. Do not hold yourself back by staying in relationships that inhibit your growth. Honor yourself by choosing relationships that reflect where you are now.

MESSAGES FOR MOVING FORWARD

Changing Your Life
May Require Changing Your Relationships

You may have to walk away from relationships
where you do not feel valued, loved, and accepted.
You may also need to create a shift in your relational patterns
and your communication.
Remember, this is not exclusive to romantic partners.
Allow yourself space to refresh, rework,
and revise relationships with friends and family too!
People grow and people change.
It is amazing and wonderful!
However, not everyone changes in the same way or at the same time.
Do not hold yourself back by staying
in relationships that inhibit your growth.
Honor yourself by choosing relationships
that reflect where you are now.

MY PROCESS OF HEALING

his is the part everyone wants to know. Everyone wants to know how I did it, how did I heal?

When we are hurting, it's natural to want a quick prescription or a magic bullet or an instant cure.

I would love to come clean and give you the miraculous formula for healing. I really wish I had that. The reality is that a wide variety of things brought me to a place of deeper healing, and I employed many strategies to get to this place.

I repeat: There is not any one thing I did that worked. The answer is that there were many elements and layers to healing. Different things work for different people and some situations require different approaches. I do think that you have to find what works for you, but I also know how difficult it can be to find that.

While I had to go through many crises, traumas, and stressful events for me to reach my breaking point, my hope is that you will notice some of your patterns and heal more quickly than I did. I truly believe that while I worked toward healing for decades, I was only ever halfway healed. I was unable to attain the healing and wholeness I sought due to not fully understanding my deep core issues. I believe I would have healed more quickly if I had achieved that understanding much sooner. I am a huge advocate for people to use their voices and speak their truth(s). Staying silent, holding things in, and not addressing trauma properly were detrimental to my life in so many ways.

It is important to note that because of all of the situations I've lived through, I have had many "opportunities" to try a wide variety of therapies, prescriptions, and healing treatments. I have spent the majority of my life trying to heal. I have been mostly successful at it, which is why I have a hard time telling any person to do one thing. I had to do many things over a variety of years to get myself to the point where I could go back to face old wounds.

I have tried different versions of therapy in a variety of contexts, through various practitioners, and over the course of several decades. When we experienced family trauma, I went to therapy. When I had issues in college, I went to therapy and took anti-depressants and anti-anxiety meds. When I experienced infertility, I went to therapy, sat in a few support groups, and wrote about it in grad school. When I had marital issues, I went to couples and individual counseling. When I was dealing with lupus, I went to therapy again. After my divorce, I returned to therapy.

See what that is? Going to therapy, over and over? That is a pattern too. I have repeatedly recognized when I needed another person to listen. I have routinely sought out help for my mental health, knowing that something was there for me to work through.

During different times, I have been on medications for anxiety, depression, post-traumatic stress disorder, attention deficit disorder, and I'm sure other things I do not even remember. I have tried several medication combinations in an effort to improve my mental health. Depending on the situation, some were helpful for periods of time. While I do not need them in this current space, I may in the future.

I do prefer to go the holistic route when possible, but I personally know and recognize the value of some pharmaceuticals. I hate the side effects and how much they cost, but if I needed them, I would still take them. I do think the various therapies and medications would have worked better had I really been going back to the root issue and talked about my abuse years ago.

I am well aware that good mental health care can be hard to find. I had been through psychiatrists, counselors, and psychologists before.

This time, I felt stuck.

I could not get in to see someone as quickly as I felt I needed to. Many doctors were not accepting new patients. Others were but did not take Medicare. Even with my work insurance, on top of that, some co-pays were several hundred dollars for a new patient.

I did not have that kind of money. I could not front the money and think of battling with my insurance company for reimbursement. I was already dealing with car and health insurance companies from the crash. I did not freaking have time to keep calling and begging to be seen.

I was not suicidal. I was not a danger to myself physically, however I knew I was in crisis. I needed help. I did not know where to turn.

So, I went to the community mental health clinic. You know, the type of clinic where you bring all your documentation, show up before they open, wait in line, and hope you are called to be seen. I had to go several times before I could get to the right person.

One time, in particular, I was close to hysterical. I could

feel myself spiraling, and I knew how bad things were. I knew that I had to get through these memories. I knew I needed trauma therapy. I told them about the car crash and my panic. It took me several, and I do mean several, visits to tell anyone about the abuse.

None of this should read as a slam on this, or any other, community mental health facility. In my experience, these centers are understaffed. The workers are severely underpaid and have a great amount of strain placed upon them. I am incredibly thankful I had a center in my town. I am lucky that I have a flexible work schedule and I was able to do this.

Thankfully, I was able to start seeing a psychiatrist. She prescribed some short-acting anti-anxiety meds, ADHD meds, and anti-depressants. I had been on all of them before, so I wasn't worried about any of it, but I also did not want to take any of it. I used the short-acting anti-anxiety meds to ward off panic attacks. I went on and off the other meds and did not feel they were what I needed at this time.

By this point, I was very open about where I was in trying to heal from the sexual abuse. I was really concerned about entering trauma therapy, but no trauma therapist was available the entire time I was a patient at the community mental health center. They work hard and help many people, but they can only help when they have the funds and resources to do so.

In a strange way, I was thankful that I'd had to heal from crisis and trauma before. I knew that I was safe, even as I felt panic. I did not need to seek care over someone who was a danger to themselves, so I kept my psychiatrist there and started searching for counselors.

I completed workbooks, checked textbooks out of the university library, and went back to therapy as much as I could afford to—which was rarely. I also tried several alternative therapies and went to different healing practitioners. I knew I needed to learn to calm my mind. I wanted to go about this through multiple channels. I wanted to hit it from many angles.

I went to reiki courses and attended a series of chakra classes with a local shaman. I loved being at these and learned how to re-center and ground myself. I attended healing circles, went to prayer groups, attended support groups, and took online meditation classes.

I learned the emotional freedom technique with a therapist who led me through the pressure points and ways to reduce the physical sensation surrounding my traumatic events. And I started journaling again. This was one of the best tools for processing my thoughts and feelings, and this became the single biggest comfort in my healing.

There was a lot I could not afford. I wanted to go to more classes, and I wanted to go to more therapy. I wanted to do a lot of things. Even with insurance, the co-pays were often more than my budget allowed.

So, I had to do other things too. I listened to a lot of soothing music. I took a lot of Epsom salt baths, and I did a lot of deep breathing. I spent time outdoors and reconnected with nature.

I already owned paddleboards, and I live in a city with two rivers. I went and sat by the water and let myself be still whenever possible. I also have mature trees in my backyard. I went and sat underneath them and walked around barefoot in the grass.

Please keep in mind, I also read about relationships, feelings, communication, and psychology, A LOT. I did what I knew how to do from years of going to school and reading research. I do research for my lectures and classes, and because I am teaching at a university, I have access to a lot of wonderful textbooks and academic journals. Every time I prepared a lecture, I thought more deeply about how I could utilize the research to better my own life, in addition to that of my students.

The combination of my years of therapy for everything else, coupled with my education and concepts and skills I have taught, made me hyper-aware of what I had to do to heal. I really did work at this. I still do—for me, it is part of self-care.

Self-care means recognizing the good you are doing for your body. So, figure out the things you need to do for your body. I did not just read about all of these things. I actually practiced them daily and still do.

I am big on mindfulness, meditation, and journaling. I began to see myself for who I was instead of merely being a reflection of all the things I should be. As I go through my day, I thank myself for completing tasks, and I practice positive self-talk.

Here is my morning practice of self-care: I wake up and pray, meditate, and journal. Journaling is one space where I get in touch with my needs and work through my feelings. This is a way I clear my head and set my daily intentions. I think about my tasks for the day and try to start from a peaceful place.

I have used writing as a tool to get through crisis and trauma before, but this time I returned to it as a daily practice. Even if I was feeling completely amazing. I picked up a notebook and started journaling again right away in the morning before I would even get out of bed. I would dump everything that was in my brain and write down anything I could remember from the night before. Even if nothing monumental emerges through this process, I feel like I've accomplished something before I even get out of bed. I did not feel that way when I picked up my phone and scrolled through social media upon waking!

I also like to journal at night to process the day. I often take notes throughout the day to remind myself what I want to look at further. Sometimes, that is more comforting to me than writing, so I will speak notes into my phone.

I often talk out loud to myself as a processing tool. There are some things that I need to write and also say out loud, so I actually talk to myself quite a bit and feel it is high underrated and maligned. I do have a few friends I reach out to who let me say whatever I need to. They know I do not want or need to hash things out but, rather, I just want and need to be heard and talk about what's going on with me.

In my journal, I work to trace my feelings. Ok, so I am sad. Do I know why? Was it an event? What about the event? I keep asking myself enough questions so that I am processing deeper layers of where the feeling comes from.

Pretend you're talking to a 2-year-old. Keep asking yourself why. If you don't know the answer, write about that. Explore the possibilities. Is this a common trigger for you? Are these feelings that creep up repeatedly?

Use your journal as data. What themes or patterns are you stuck in? How are you creating a space that reflects these situations?

Usually my feelings lead back to a need. It is why I tell my students to know their needs and let their feelings follow. If I go first with the feeling, I may not know what I am really seeking.

Take time for yourself mentally, physically, spiritually, emotionally, and creatively. When I care for myself, I am more productive on tasks I might not find as enjoyable. For example, I don't love paying bills, but it is much less stressful when I am in an emotionally calm state versus when I'm frantic and stressed.

When I teach, I use examples with my students about how I have fallen and gotten back up. I have used my voice to teach college students for years. What I have found is people do want to talk, but they need to feel safe when they do.

I am so lucky to be in a position where I have created safe spaces for my students. I have seen them open up about abusive relationships, toxic family members, health issues, money concerns, you name it. They do this in my classes because we work hard to create a climate of respect. I am honored to have been privy to those moments of transformation.

I am humbled that I have seen the compassion of others as they reach out to console a classmate or offer up advice based on personal history. All these things take courage. They take vulnerability. They take trust. That is what happens in my classrooms.

So, what does your safe space look like? Is it your friends? The thing with friendship is you also need to ensure you are not overburdening those closest to you.

I tell my students all the time, ask someone before you unload. I used to unload like crazy. I learned to ask people if they were available to talk and ensure they were in the frame of mind to be supportive. Just because we may heal best through talking doesn't mean everyone has to listen. It is important to find the people who want to listen and are able to do so in a way that works for them too.

Perhaps, talking is not your thing, and you hate writing. Maybe for you, it is an app or a space where you can quiet your mind. Do you like to paint, draw, or sing? For some, it might be a long drive, while for others it might going for a run.

Active hobbies and past times are great, but you need to make sure you are actually processing those emotions too. I love my paddleboard because when I am on the water it helps me clear my head and think through things. That is different than going paddle boarding with friends for exercise. Recognize how you give your mind space to process. It is different than leisure time and needs to be treated as such.

Make an appointment with yourself and treat it as the most important thing on your calendar. Value yourself enough to make your mental health a priority. Do whatever it is that gets you to really be still in your mind so you can reflect and process. I could not go to the gym for years. I had to build up to a place where I could be physically active again. I started with stretching, walking, and yoga at home. We all know how helpful exercise is to improve physical and mental health, so if you are physically able, get out there and do it!

First you know your needs. Flexibility is different than completely bending or breaking. Yes, work with relational partners but, first, make sure you are solid on your own needs and desires. If you bend, make sure it is a communicated compromise that you can live with. You do not get to be angry or resentful at someone else if you are the one who changed the boundary and said it was acceptable.

Do you know what else? You have control over who you let into your life. Again, are you assessing your needs? How can you find better balance for your life?

For me, that means no longer chasing balance. I realize that my life is full of ups and downs. There isn't a way to fit in everything in equal amounts. Some days that means I work for 14 hours and I forget to eat. Other days I spend the whole day on Netflix. Sometimes, my kids' activities overwhelm the schedule.

I am learning to respect the rhythms of my own

productivity. I don't beat myself up for what someone else might think I should be doing, and I stopped beating myself up for what I "should be" doing. I no longer chase balance. Instead, I reflect and strive to realign my priorities and schedule so that I can have a sloth day when I need it and not feel one ounce of guilt.

I understand this is a place of privilege, and I get that I am fortunate to have a break from work where I can have this restoration. I don't believe we always take true ownership over how we self-sabotage. I know I don't. I get frantic, burned out, overwhelmed, and exhausted. I look for balance and get angry I don't have more time to do all the things that are on my plate every day. So, I'm actively taking stock of the little things I can do to make each day more peaceful.

How can you be balanced if you don't protect your energy? For me, it always goes back to those boundaries.

It was vital for me to get stronger boundaries. How do *you* establish boundaries? Yes, I know, I already wrote about this, but I'm saying it again.

What is your yes?

What is your no?

Are you clear on these?

Do you bend for others?

Are you protecting your time and energy?

A note to parents: Putting your kids before yourself is unhealthy. If you have not healed yourself, you are placing generational trauma on them. Heal yourself so you can raise healthier kids.

Get out the paper. Have your kids draw their feelings and ask them about what they drew. Draw yours along with them. Show your children that processing and discussing emotions is healthy. Model the behavior by showing them various ways to work through emotions. Using your voice doesn't have to mean talking. Make a sculpture out of clay, paint a picture, do breathing exercises, and above all, meet them where they are.

Many of you might simply have too many commitments. Are there things you can stop doing? I stopped saying yes to things that I could say no to. It turns out there was a lot I could say no to. I wouldn't have believed you if you would have told me. I thought I had to do everything. I thought I had to, or someone would be disappointed or upset. Guess what? It doesn't matter if someone else is disappointed or upset. If I am staying true to my authentic self and I am choosing what is best for my emotional health, that is the number one concern.

Other people's reactions to your boundaries are their responsibility, not yours. Again, remember, you do not change yourself because of someone else's feelings!

There is another big piece I want to address about how to heal. Part of healing is recognizing that bad things happen. Part of healing is recognizing that all the emotions are important.

I have been teaching about this for years: You do not need to be happy all the time. We can talk about our hardships without it meaning that we are melting down or in need of an intervention. It is unfortunate that when people do try to be real and vulnerable, they are sometimes made to feel as though they are weak.

After I started my social media accounts and started talking about what I do in the classroom, I made it a point to talk about my bad days. You can be a life coach, a relationship coach, a counselor, or a doctor and still have bad days. You can be completely emotionally healthy and still feel sad. It does not make you weak or pathetic.

We need to understand what recovery looks like.

Recovery from trauma, stress, crisis, relational turbulence, hardship, etc.

You might still be sad.

You might still question if you are on the right path.

You may feel like you are broken.

All of that is perfectly acceptable. It is part of the process. Healing is continual work and it takes real effort. Vulnerability and emotion are real. Holding things in is lying by omission and fake as fuck. I think there is strength in emotion. I find vulnerability inspiring.

Being vulnerable and open is not a cry for help.

It's a testament to my emotional strength.

Stop trying to save me. I saved myself.

This is not a cry for help, it's a rallying cry.

What if we made emotional openness and vulnerability the norm? What if talking about your broken pieces could help you feel more whole? What if the compassion you received from others really was helpful? Because you felt safe? What would it take for you to realize you are whole? Are there therapies available that you can draw upon?

In what areas can you grow more? Are you fulfilling your needs, desires, hopes, and dreams?

Are there practical ways you can regain control over your happiness?

What 3 things can you do to be nice to yourself today?

What small steps can you take toward a large goal?

My hope is that you will take this book and analyze your own patterns and habits. We often judge ourselves based on our darkest moments and internalize our smallest mistakes. Release that pain and the story that caused it. Feel it. Neutralize it. Let it Go.

CONCLUSION

I never thought I would write this story. I never thought I could share this truth. I finally realized that once I was willing to work through my own pain, I could more effectively help others. The ways in which I felt broken used to overwhelm me. My emotions overtook me—fear, anger, resentment, guilt, shame, blame—all of what I carried surrounding my abuse is now gone. I may never experience complete healing according to the standards of some, but I will always know I am whole.

Although the year 2018 brought many bad things to the surface, to wish it hadn't happened would be to cast away the important transformation and spiritual growth that came along with it.

I am a survivor of childhood sexual abuse.

If I had received services from an advocacy center, I might have learned how to combat the coping mechanisms and patterns I created to survive the abuse. If I had been able to talk about what happened many years before I was actually able to, it would have greatly aided and expedited my healing.

Time can heal, giving the restorative space necessary to repair that which is broken. It has taken a lifetime to undo the core beliefs my abuser instilled in me. I have hurt people with my brokenness time and time again. I have made poor choices, bad decisions, and have not always been my most authentic self.

Yet, societally and individually, we often seek to calm and nullify any turbulence or feelings other than happiness.

Guess what?

You can be one hundred percent emotionally healthy and still feel sadness. Or anger. Or shame. This does not make you unstable. Feeling everything, processing it, and letting it go is what makes you emotionally healthy. When you choose to shut out your feelings or shove your emotions aside, all you are doing is reinjuring yourself.

All emotions are healthy.

You are complex.

You are loved.

You are healed.

You are whole.

I do not blame my abuser for my choices, but I do carry the weight of every mental seed he planted. He stole so much from me and robbed me of critical stages of development. I was not on track emotionally. I was way ahead of the curve physically. Through an adult lens and while raising my children, I now realize how devastating his abuse and its aftermath were on my development. By processing and releasing the things he did to me—the things he said to me and about me—I have been able to grow into the person I should have been allowed to be.

I have also grown as a teacher. It is my wish for my story to stand alongside many others who have shared their truths. As such, my overarching goal is to continue to build a platform for other voices to be heard. I have changed the way I teach at the college level and have developed workshops and speaking events in a continued effort to create a space where others can share their stories.

Having written this, I acknowledge that there are many others who speak of being broken. Many books seem to say exactly what I want to say. I hear many speakers presenting the same ideas I wish to share. But I am not afraid to repeat what anyone else is saying.

I needed to write this to find myself—to get to a place of deeper healing. I wanted to own my story. I want you to own yours. I applaud anyone who shares their voice, be it on social media, via text, or on a global scale. The more people who are talking about healing, vulnerability, bravery, courage, and openness, the better.

I want to shine a bright light on all of us who have broken pieces. My goal is for people to feel safe to talk about their hardships without fear. Find me on social media, send me an email, or find another platform to talk about your pieces and share what makes you whole. Through the exploration of our feelings and through communication about our own journeys we can enlighten, entertain, and educate.

We can show others they are not alone. We can all create a safer space for emotions to be fully expressed. There really is strength in numbers. Bringing together all our stories creates wholeness and healing. It is important to look at the interconnected whole of each life and the being whole that we should draw upon. We grow stronger when we recognize we are not alone.

We can all heal together.

We each have our own story. Our stories keep us vibrant and healthy. The jagged pieces do not have to destroy us. The scars, the sadness, and the traumas make us whole.

ACKNOWLEDGMENTS

Thank you to all the people who have seen my broken pieces and loved me anyway. Thank you for seeing me as whole, even when I could not.

To my friends: Thank you for being there in the various stages of my existence.

To my students: Thank you for your encouragement, support, and hard work.

To my family: Thank you. For believing, seeing, and nurturing my inner sparkle and authentic self from the very beginning.

A SPECIAL THANKS

Thank you to the many individuals who read various versions of this book: I appreciate your feedback and insight. I value your comments, questions, and suggestions. I am thankful for your time and energy.

Dr. Cassandra LeClair is an author, professor, communication consultant, and motivational speaker. She is an expert on communicating feelings and improving connections.

Cassandra's mission is to educate individuals on how to have effective and healthy communication to enhance their relationships. She works to help others gain understanding of their communication practices to improve their relationships with friends and family members, in the workplace, and beyond.

Cassandra completed her Ph.D. in Communication Studies at the University of Nebraska-Lincoln, where she focused on Interpersonal and Family Communication, with a specialization in Women's and Gender studies. Dr. LeClair teaches a variety of classes at the collegiate level, where she encourages her students to explore their own patterns and improve their communication. Her teaching and research interests fuel her campus and community involvement. She is active in many local organizations that seek to empower and educate individuals on relationships and identity.

Cassandra lives in New Braunfels, Texas with her two children.

Stay in touch! connect@cassandraleclair.com

To learn more visit: www.CassandraLeClair.com

facebook.com/DrCassandraLeClair
instagram.com/DrCassandraLeClair

Made in the USA
Lexington, KY
15 December 2019